ZURICH
TRAVEL GUIDE
2023-2024

THE ULTIMATE TRAVEL GUIDE OF SEOUL

GRIFFIN G. MEIER

ZURICH TRAVEL GUIDE 2023-2024
The Ultimate Travel Guide of Switzerland.

© Griffin G. Meier
© E.G.P. Editorial

Printed in USA.
ISBN-13: 9798392425518

Copyright © All rights reserved.

ZURICH
TRAVEL GUIDE

THE MOST POPULAR PLACES IN ZURICH

In the heart of Europe, where mountains cradle a vibrant city, Zurich hums with the echoes of its medieval past and the buzzing whispers of its cosmopolitan present. A blend of the old and the new, Zurich is a treasure trove waiting to be unearthed by the inquisitive traveler. Our sojourn begins on cobblestone streets, meandering through the nooks and crannies of history, where each turn reveals a hidden gem, a story steeped in the centuries.

Within these pages, we delve into the cultural fabric that makes Zurich a haven for art connoisseurs and history aficionados. From the hallowed halls of museums to the dynamic spaces of galleries, the city's spirit is captured in the brushstrokes of the masters and the avant-garde. The lights of theaters and the laughter of children fill the air as we explore the city's stage for performing arts and the playgrounds designed for young minds.

We wander the paths less traveled, embarking on tours and walks that showcase the city's unique character, its fusion of tradition and modernity. Let us marvel at the architectural wonders that have withstood the test of time, whispering tales of the past in their stony silence.

As the sun begins to set, we uncover the secrets of Zurich's culinary scene, sampling the delights that await the discerning palate, in establishments revered and undiscovered. And as night falls, the city comes alive with the pulse of its vibrant nightlife, a testament to the joy of living in this enchanting metropolis.

Allow this book to be your guide, an invitation to explore and experience the enchantment that lies within the heart of Switzerland. Delve into the rich tapestry of Zurich's attractions, shops, museums, theaters, galleries, tours, walks, places for kids, restaurants, and nightlife spots.

Happy travels!

TABLE OF CONTENTS

ATTRACTIONS	7
SHOPS	17
MUSEUMS	27
THEATERS	37
GALLERIES	49
TOURS	59
WALKS	69
KIDS	80
RESTAURANTS	93
NIGHTLIFE	103
COMPLETE LIST	115

ATTRACTIONS

GROSSMÜNSTER

Address: Grossmünsterplatz, 8001 Zurich, Switzerland

Historical background: The Grossmünster is a Romanesque-style church that was built in the 12th century. It is one of the most important landmarks of Zurich and has been the center of the Swiss Reformation.

Curiosity and facts: The Grossmünster is known for its two towers, which are not symmetrical. One tower is slightly taller than the other, and this is said to symbolize the difference between the right and wrong paths in life.

Practical information: The Grossmünster is open to visitors every day, except on certain holidays. Guided tours are available, and there is a small fee to enter the church.

Highlights and must-sees: The stained glass windows by artist Sigmar Polke are a must-see, as well as the beautiful views from the tower.

Cost: There is a fee of CHF 5 for adults to enter the church.

Quality: The Grossmünster is a well-maintained church with a rich history and beautiful architecture.

Advice: Visitors should plan to spend at least an hour exploring the church and taking in the views from the tower.

Getting there: The Grossmünster is located in the heart of Zurich and is easily accessible by foot or public transportation.

Nearby attractions: The Fraumünster, Lake Zurich, Bahnhofstrasse, and Niederdorf are all within walking distance of the Grossmünster.

FRAUMÜNSTER

Address: Münsterhof, 8001 Zurich, Switzerland

Historical background: The Fraumünster is a Gothic-style church that was built in the 13th century. It is one of the most famous landmarks in Zurich and is known for its beautiful stained glass windows.

Curiosity and facts: The Fraumünster was originally a convent for noblewomen, and it has been a church since the Reformation. The stained glass windows were created by artist Marc Chagall in 1970.

Practical information: The Fraumünster is open to visitors every day, except on certain holidays. Guided tours are available, and there is a small fee to enter the church.

Highlights and must-sees: The stained glass windows by Marc Chagall are a must-see, as well as the beautiful views from the tower.

Cost: There is a fee of CHF 5 for adults to enter the church.

Quality: The Fraumünster is a well-maintained church with a rich history and beautiful architecture.

Advice: Visitors should plan to spend at least an hour exploring the church and taking in the views from the tower.

Getting there: The Fraumünster is located in the heart of Zurich and is easily accessible by foot or public transportation.

Nearby attractions: The Grossmünster, Lake Zurich, Bahnhofstrasse, and Niederdorf are all within walking distance of the Fraumünster.

BAHNHOFSTRASSE

Address: Bahnhofstrasse, 8001 Zurich, Switzerland

Historical background: Bahnhofstrasse is one of the most famous shopping streets in Switzerland. It was built in the late 19th century and has been a popular shopping destination ever since.

Curiosity and facts: Bahnhofstrasse is considered one of the most expensive shopping streets in the world, with high-end luxury brands and designer boutiques.

Practical information: Bahnhofstrasse is open every day, and there are many shops, restaurants, and cafes to explore.

Highlights and must-sees: Visitors should check out the luxury shopping, and stop by the Paradeplatz for the iconic view of the financial district.

Cost: Shopping in Bahnhofstrasse can be expensive, but there are also plenty of budget-friendly options available.

Quality: Bahnhofstrasse is known for its high-end luxury shopping and top-quality products.

Advice: Visitors should bring comfortable shoes, as there is a lot of ground to cover on Bahnhofstrasse.

Getting there: Bahnhofstrasse is located in the heart of Zurich and is easily accessible by foot or public transportation.

Nearby attractions: Lake Zurich, Grossmünster, Fraumünster, and Niederdorf are all within walking distance of Bahnhofstrasse.

LAKE ZURICH

Address: Lake Zurich, 8001 Zurich, Switzerland

Historical background: Lake Zurich is a large lake in the heart of Switzerland. It has been a popular tourist destination for centuries and is known for its stunning scenery and outdoor activities.

Curiosity and facts: Lake Zurich is surrounded by beautiful mountains and is a popular destination for swimming, boating, and other water sports.

Practical information: Lake Zurich is open to visitors every day, and there are many public beaches and parks to enjoy. There are also boat tours available, as well as rental options for boats and water equipment.

Highlights and must-sees: Visitors should take a boat tour of the lake and enjoy the beautiful views of the mountains and surrounding cities. The Uetliberg is also a must-visit, with its scenic hiking trails and panoramic views of the lake.

Cost: Access to the lake and public beaches is free, but boat tours and equipment rentals may have a fee.

Quality: Lake Zurich is a high-quality tourist destination known for its stunning scenery and outdoor activities.

Advice: Visitors should bring sunscreen, a hat, and plenty of water, especially during the summer months.

Getting there: Lake Zurich is located in the heart of Zurich and is easily accessible by foot or public transportation.

Nearby attractions: The Grossmünster, Fraumünster, Bahnhofstrasse, Niederdorf, and Uetliberg are all within close proximity of Lake Zurich.

UETLIBERG

Address: Uetliberg, 8045 Zurich, Switzerland

Historical background: The Uetliberg is a mountain located on the outskirts of Zurich. It is a popular destination for hiking and offers panoramic views of the city and Lake Zurich.

Curiosity and facts: The Uetliberg is the highest point in the Zurich area, and is a popular spot for stargazing and taking in the sunset.

Practical information: The Uetliberg is open to visitors every day, and there are several hiking trails to explore. There is also a train that runs from the city center to the top of the mountain.

Highlights and must-sees: Visitors should hike to the top of the mountain and take in the panoramic views of the city and Lake Zurich. The sunset is also a must-see, as it provides a stunning view of the surrounding landscape.

Cost: There is a fee for the train ride to the top of the Uetliberg, but hiking is free.

Quality: The Uetliberg is a high-quality tourist destination known for its stunning views and outdoor activities.

Advice: Visitors should bring comfortable hiking shoes, plenty of water, and a jacket as the temperature can be cooler on the mountain.

Getting there: The Uetliberg is located on the outskirts of Zurich and is easily accessible by train from the city center.

Nearby attractions: Lake Zurich, Lindenhof, and the Zurich Opera House are all within close proximity of the Uetliberg.

LINDENHOF

Address: Lindenhof, 8001 Zurich, Switzerland

Historical background: The Lindenhof is a park located in the heart of Zurich. It is known for its beautiful views of the city and the river Limmat.

Curiosity and facts: The Lindenhof was once a Roman fort, and is now a popular spot for picnics and outdoor recreation. It is also a popular spot for events and concerts during the summer months.

Practical information: The Lindenhof is open to visitors every day, and there are plenty of benches and picnic areas to enjoy.

Highlights and must-sees: Visitors should take in the beautiful views of the city and the river Limmat, and enjoy a picnic or a relaxing walk in the park.

Cost: Access to the Lindenhof is free.

Quality: The Lindenhof is a high-quality park known for its beautiful views and outdoor recreation opportunities.

Advice: Visitors should bring a picnic basket or snacks to enjoy in the park.

Getting there: The Lindenhof is located in the heart of Zurich and is easily accessible by foot or public transportation.

Nearby attractions: The Grossmünster, Fraumünster, Niederdorf, and Lake Zurich are all within walking distance of the Lindenhof.

NIEDERDORF

Address: Niederdorf, 8001 Zurich, Switzerland

Historical background: Niederdorf is a neighborhood in the heart of Zurich known for its vibrant nightlife, cultural scene, and unique shopping.

Curiosity and facts: Niederdorf is a popular destination for nightlife, with plenty of bars, clubs, and live music venues. It is also known for its historic architecture and cobblestone streets.

Practical information: Niederdorf is open every day, with many shops, restaurants, and bars to explore.

Highlights and must-sees: Visitors should explore the historic architecture, sample the local cuisine, and enjoy the nightlife in Niederdorf.

Cost: Shopping and dining in Niederdorf can vary in cost, but there are plenty of budget-friendly options available.

Quality: Niederdorf is a high-quality neighborhood known for its vibrant nightlife and cultural scene.

Advice: Visitors should plan to spend an evening in Niederdorf to fully experience the nightlife and cultural scene.

Getting there: Niederdorf is located in the heart of Zurich and is easily accessible by foot or public transportation.

Nearby attractions: The Grossmünster, Fraumünster, Bahnhofstrasse, Lake Zurich, and Lindenhof are all within walking distance of Niederdorf.

ZURICH OPERA HOUSE

Address: Zurich Opera House, Falkenstrasse 1, 8008 Zurich, Switzerland

Historical background: The Zurich Opera House is a cultural landmark in the city of Zurich, known for its world-class performances and stunning architecture.

Curiosity and facts: The Zurich Opera House is one of the most important cultural institutions in Switzerland and hosts a variety of performances, including operas, ballets, and concerts.

Practical information: The Zurich Opera House is open for performances and events, and tickets can be purchased in advance or on the day of the performance.

Highlights and must-sees: Visitors should attend a performance at the Zurich Opera House, and enjoy the beautiful interior and architecture of the building.

Cost: Ticket prices for performances at the Zurich Opera House vary, but there are options available for all budgets.

Quality: The Zurich Opera House is known for its high-quality performances and world-class cultural offerings.

Advice: Visitors should plan to arrive early to enjoy a drink at the bar or take a tour of the building before the performance.

Getting there: The Zurich Opera House is located in the heart of Zurich and is easily accessible by foot or public transportation.

Nearby attractions: The Grossmünster, Fraumünster, Bahnhofstrasse, Lake Zurich, and Niederdorf are all within walking distance of the Zurich Opera House.

ST. PETER'S CHURCH

Address: St. Peter's Church, St. Peterhofstatt 8, 8001 Zurich, Switzerland

Historical background: St. Peter's Church is a historic church located in the heart of Zurich. It is one of the oldest churches in the city and has a rich history and cultural significance.

Curiosity and facts: St. Peter's Church is known for its beautiful Gothic architecture and stained-glass windows. It is also a popular spot for events and concerts.

Practical information: St. Peter's Church is open to visitors every day and offers guided tours and events.

Highlights and must-sees: Visitors should take a tour of the church and enjoy the beautiful architecture and stained-glass windows.

Cost: Admission to St. Peter's Church is free, but guided tours and events may have a fee.

Quality: St. Peter's Church is a high-quality tourist destination known for its historic and cultural significance.

Advice: Visitors should plan to spend some time exploring the church and taking in its beauty.

Getting there: St. Peter's Church is located in the heart of Zurich and is easily accessible by foot or public transportation.

Nearby attractions: The Grossmünster, Fraumünster, Bahnhofstrasse, Niederdorf, and Lake Zurich are all within walking distance of St. Peter's Church.

CHINESE GARDEN ZURICH

Address: Chinese Garden Zurich, Mythenquai 2, 8002 Zurich, Switzerland

Historical background: The Chinese Garden Zurich is a beautiful garden located in the heart of Zurich. It is a replica of a traditional Chinese garden and offers a unique cultural experience.

Curiosity and facts: The Chinese Garden Zurich is the only Chinese Garden in Europe and is a popular destination for tourists and locals alike. It is known for its stunning scenery and tranquil atmosphere.

Practical information: The Chinese Garden Zurich is open to visitors every day and offers guided tours and events.

Highlights and must-sees: Visitors should take a guided tour of the garden and enjoy the beautiful scenery and unique cultural experience.

Cost: Admission to the Chinese Garden Zurich may have a fee, and guided tours may also have an additional cost.

Quality: The Chinese Garden Zurich is a high-quality tourist destination known for its beautiful scenery and unique cultural experience.

Advice: Visitors should bring a camera to capture the beauty of the garden, and plan to spend some time exploring the different areas of the garden.

Getting there: The Chinese Garden Zurich is located in the heart of Zurich and is easily accessible by foot or public transportation.

Nearby attractions: The Bahnhofstrasse, Lake Zurich, Niederdorf, and St. Peter's Church are all within walking distance of the Chinese Garden Zurich.

SHOPS

JELMOLI

Address: Bahnhofstrasse, 8021 Zurich, Switzerland.

Phone: +41 44 220 44 11

Products: High-end fashion, beauty, home decor, and gourmet food.

Hours of operation: Monday to Friday from 9:30 am to 8:00 pm, Saturday from 9:00 am to 6:00 pm.

Cost score: $$

Historical background: Jelmoli was founded in 1833 and is considered one of the oldest department stores in Switzerland. It has been a landmark in Zurich for over a century and is known for its high-end fashion and luxury goods.

Highlights and must-sees: The high-end fashion department, the beauty and fragrance section, and the gourmet food area.

Curiosity and facts: Jelmoli is known for its luxurious shopping experience and its wide range of high-end products, from fashion and beauty to home decor and gourmet food.

Advice: Plan your visit in advance to make the most of your time and budget, and be prepared to indulge in a luxurious shopping experience.

Getting there: The nearest metro station is Paradeplatz, from there it's a 5-minute walk to Jelmoli.

Nearby attractions: Bahnhofstrasse, the Lake of Zurich, and the Swiss National Museum.

GLOBUS

Address: Bahnhofstrasse, 8001 Zurich, Switzerland.

Phone: +41 44 224 24 24

Products: Fashion, beauty, home decor, and gourmet food.

Hours of operation: Monday to Friday from 9:00 am to 8:00 pm, Saturday from 9:00 am to 6:00 pm.

Cost score: $$

Historical background: Globus is a chain of department stores in Switzerland and was founded in the late 19th century. It has been a popular shopping destination in Zurich for over a century and is known for its wide range of products and affordable prices.

Highlights and must-sees: The fashion and beauty departments, the home decor section, and the gourmet food area.

Curiosity and facts: Globus is known for its affordable prices and its wide range of products, from fashion and beauty to home decor and gourmet food.

Advice: Plan your visit in advance to make the most of your time and budget, and be prepared to find great deals and a wide range of products at affordable prices.

Getting there: The nearest metro station is Paradeplatz, from there it's a 5-minute walk to Globus.

Nearby attractions: Bahnhofstrasse, the Lake of Zurich, and the Swiss National Museum.

MANOR

Address: Stauffacherstrasse, 8004 Zurich, Switzerland.

Phone: +41 44 208 88 11

Products: Fashion, beauty, home decor, and electronics.

Hours of operation: Monday to Friday from 9:00 am to 8:00 pm, Saturday from 9:00 am to 6:00 pm.

Cost score: $$

Historical background: Manor is a chain of department stores in Switzerland and was founded in the late 19th century. It has been a popular shopping destination in Zurich for over a century and is known for its wide range of products and affordable prices.

Highlights and must-sees: The fashion and beauty departments, the home decor section, and the electronics area.

Curiosity and facts: Manor is known for its affordable prices and its wide range of products, from fashion and beauty to home decor and electronics.

Advice: Plan your visit in advance to make the most of your time and budget, and be prepared to find great deals and a wide range of products at affordable prices.

Getting there: The nearest metro station is Stauffacher, from there it's a 5-minute walk to Manor.

Nearby attractions: Bahnhofstrasse, the Lake of Zurich, and the Swiss National Museum.

BÜRKLIPLATZ MARKET

Address: Bürkliplatz, 8008 Zurich, Switzerland.

Products: Fresh produce, flowers, and handmade goods.

Hours of operation: Monday to Saturday from 6:00 am to 6:00 pm.

Cost score: $

Historical background: The Bürkliplatz Market has been a staple in Zurich for over a century and is known for its fresh produce, flowers, and handmade goods. It is a popular destination for locals and tourists alike.

Highlights and must-sees: The fresh produce, flowers, and handmade goods sections, and the vibrant atmosphere of the market.

Curiosity and facts: The Bürkliplatz Market is known for its fresh produce, flowers, and handmade goods, and is a great place to find unique and locally made products. It is also a hub for local farmers and small businesses to sell their goods.

Advice: Go early in the morning for the best selection and freshest produce, and be prepared to haggle for the best prices.

Getting there: The nearest metro station is Bürkliplatz, from there it's a 2-minute walk to the market.

Nearby attractions: Lake Zurich, the Swiss National Museum, and the Old Town of Zurich.

SPRÜNGLI

Address: Paradeplatz, 8001 Zurich, Switzerland.

Phone: +41 44 224 46 46

Products: Confectionery, chocolate, and pastries.

Hours of operation: Monday to Friday from 7:30 am to 7:00 pm, Saturday from 9:00 am to 6:00 pm.

Cost score: $$

Historical background: Sprüngli was founded in 1836 and is considered one of the oldest confectioneries in Switzerland. It is known for its high-quality chocolate, pastries, and confectionery and has been a staple in Zurich for over a century.

Highlights and must-sees: The chocolate and confectionery counters, the pastry selection, and the famous "Luxemburgerli" macarons.

Curiosity and facts: Sprüngli is known for its exceptional quality and its wide range of delicious confectionery and chocolate products. It is also a popular destination for locals and tourists alike, who come to indulge in its sweet treats and enjoy a cup of coffee or tea.

Advice: Be prepared for a long wait during peak hours and plan your visit in advance to make the most of your time and budget.

Getting there: The nearest metro station is Paradeplatz, from there it's a 2-minute walk to Sprüngli.

Nearby attractions: Bahnhofstrasse, the Lake of Zurich, and the Swiss National Museum.

GRIEDER

Address: Bahnhofstrasse, 8001 Zurich, Switzerland.

Phone: +41 44 221 11 11

Products: High-end fashion and accessories.

Hours of operation: Monday to Friday from 9:30 am to 8:00 pm, Saturday from 9:00 am to 6:00 pm.

Cost score: $$$

Historical background: Grieder was founded in the early 20th century and is considered one of the oldest high-end fashion stores in Switzerland. It is known for its exclusive fashion and accessories and has been a staple in Zurich for over a century.

Highlights and must-sees: The high-end fashion department, the accessories section, and the luxurious shopping experience.

Curiosity and facts: Grieder is known for its exceptional quality and its wide range of exclusive fashion and accessories products. It is a popular destination for those looking for luxury and high-end fashion items.

Advice: Plan your visit in advance to make the most of your time and budget, and be prepared to indulge in a luxurious shopping experience.

Getting there: The nearest metro station is Paradeplatz, from there it's a 5-minute walk to Grieder.

Nearby attractions: Bahnhofstrasse, the Lake of Zurich, and the Swiss National Museum.

COOP CITY

Address: Bahnhofstrasse, 8001 Zurich, Switzerland.

Phone: +41 44 221 11 11

Products: Fashion, beauty, home decor, electronics, and groceries.

Hours of operation: Monday to Friday from 9:00 am to 8:00 pm, Saturday from 9:00 am to 6:00 pm.

Cost score: $

Historical background: Coop City is a chain of department stores in Switzerland and was founded in the late 19th century. It has been a popular shopping destination in Zurich for over a century and is known for its wide range of products and affordable prices.

Highlights and must-sees: The fashion and beauty departments, the home decor section, the electronics area, and the grocery section.

Curiosity and facts: Coop City is known for its affordable prices and its wide range of products, from fashion and beauty to home decor, electronics, and groceries.

Advice: Plan your visit in advance to make the most of your time and budget, and be prepared to find great deals and a wide range of products at affordable prices.

Getting there: The nearest metro station is Paradeplatz, from there it's a 5-minute walk to Coop City.

Nearby attractions: Bahnhofstrasse, the Lake of Zurich, and the Swiss National Museum.

ORELL FÜSSLI

Address: Bahnhofstrasse, 8001 Zurich, Switzerland.

Phone: +41 44 224 22 11

Products: Books, stationery, and gifts.

Hours of operation: Monday to Friday from 9:00 am to 8:00 pm, Saturday from 9:00 am to 6:00 pm.

Cost score: $$

Historical background: Orell Füssli was founded in the late 17th century and is considered one of the oldest bookstores in Switzerland. It is known for its wide selection of books, stationery, and gifts and has been a staple in Zurich for over a century.

Highlights and must-sees: The book selection, the stationery department, and the gift section.

Curiosity and facts: Orell Füssli is known for its wide range of products and its exceptional selection of books, stationery, and gifts. It is a popular destination for those looking for unique and high-quality products.

Advice: Plan your visit in advance to make the most of your time and budget, and be prepared to find a wide range of products for all your book, stationery, and gift needs.

Getting there: The nearest metro station is Paradeplatz, from there it's a 5-minute walk to Orell Füssli.

Nearby attractions: Bahnhofstrasse, the Lake of Zurich, and the Swiss National Museum.

FREITAG TOWER

Address: Geroldstrasse, 8005 Zurich, Switzerland.

Phone: +41 43 243 10 10

Products: Eco-friendly bags and accessories.

Hours of operation: Monday to Friday from 10:00 am to 7:00 pm, Saturday from 10:00 am to 6:00 pm.

Cost score: $$

Historical background: Freitag Tower is a store specializing in eco-friendly bags and accessories, founded in the early 21st century. It is known for its unique and sustainable products and has become a popular destination for those looking for eco-friendly products in Zurich.

Highlights and must-sees: The eco-friendly bag selection, the accessories department, and the unique and sustainable products offered.

Curiosity and facts: Freitag Tower is known for its commitment to sustainability and its wide range of eco-friendly products. It is a popular destination for those looking for environmentally conscious products in Zurich.

Advice: Plan your visit in advance to make the most of your time and budget, and be prepared to find unique and sustainable products for all your eco-friendly needs.

Getting there: The nearest metro station is Hardbrücke, from there it's a 10-minute walk to Freitag Tower.

Nearby attractions: The Zurich Zoo, the Swiss National Museum, and the Limmat River.

CONFISERIE TEUSCHER

Address: Bahnhofstrasse, 8001 Zurich, Switzerland.

Phone: +41 43 211 11 11

Products: Confectionery, chocolate, and truffles.

Hours of operation: Monday to Friday from 9:00 am to 8:00 pm, Saturday from 9:00 am to 6:00 pm.

Cost score: $$

Historical background: Confiserie Teuscher was founded in the early 20th century and is considered one of the finest confectioneries in Switzerland. It is known for its exceptional quality chocolate, truffles, and confectionery and has been a staple in Zurich for over a century.

Highlights and must-sees: The chocolate and confectionery counters, the truffle selection, and the famous champagne truffles.

Curiosity and facts: Confiserie Teuscher is known for its exceptional quality and its wide range of delicious chocolate and confectionery products. It is a popular destination for locals and tourists alike, who come to indulge in its sweet treats and take home a box of its famous truffles.

Advice: Be prepared for a long wait during peak hours and plan your visit in advance to make the most of your time and budget.

Getting there: The nearest metro station is Paradeplatz, from there it's a 5-minute walk to Confiserie Teuscher.

Nearby attractions: Bahnhofstrasse, the Lake of Zurich, and the Swiss National Museum.

MUSEUMS

SWISS NATIONAL MUSEUM

Address: Museumstrasse 2, 8005 Zürich, Switzerland.

Phone: +41 44 218 65 11.

Exhibitions and collections: Swiss National Museum showcases the cultural and historical heritage of Switzerland and its people. The collections range from prehistory to contemporary art and design.

Admission fees and hours of operation: Admission fees for adults are CHF 16. The museum is open from 10:00 AM to 5:00 PM from Tuesday to Sunday.

Historical background: Swiss National Museum was founded in 1898 and has since been the main repository of Swiss cultural heritage. The museum is housed in a historic building, which was once the country's largest arsenal.

Highlights and must-sees: Some of the must-see exhibitions at Swiss National Museum include the collections of Swiss folk art, the Prehistory section, and the Swiss Historical Society's collection of historical objects and documents.

Curiosity and facts: Swiss National Museum is one of the largest and most comprehensive museums in Switzerland, with over 1.5 million objects in its collections.

Advice: It is recommended to allocate at least 2-3 hours to fully explore the Swiss National Museum.

Getting there: Swiss National Museum is located in the heart of Zurich, within walking distance of the main railway station. From the main railway station, take the exit towards Bahnhofstrasse and walk straight ahead until you reach the museum.

Nearby attractions: Some of the nearby attractions include Bahnhofstrasse, Lake Zurich, and the Old Town.

KUNSTHAUS ZURICH

Address: Heimplatz 1, 8002 Zürich, Switzerland.

Phone: +41 44 253 84 84.

Exhibitions and collections: Kunsthaus Zurich is one of the leading art museums in Switzerland, showcasing a wide range of exhibitions and collections of international art, from the Middle Ages to contemporary art.

Admission fees and hours of operation: Admission fees for adults are CHF 18. The museum is open from 10:00 AM to 6:00 PM from Tuesday to Sunday.

Historical background: Kunsthaus Zurich was founded in 1910 and is housed in a historic building in the heart of Zurich. The museum has been a leading institution for art in Switzerland for over a century.

Highlights and must-sees: Some of the must-see exhibitions at Kunsthaus Zurich include the collections of Swiss and international art, contemporary art, and photography.

Curiosity and facts: Kunsthaus Zurich is known for its iconic blue façade, which has become a symbol of the city.

Advice: It is recommended to allocate at least 2-3 hours to fully explore Kunsthaus Zurich.

Getting there: Kunsthaus Zurich is located in the heart of Zurich, within walking distance of the main railway station. From the main railway station, take the exit towards Bahnhofstrasse and walk straight ahead until you reach the museum.

Nearby attractions: Some of the nearby attractions include Bahnhofstrasse, Lake Zurich, and the Old Town.

RIETBERG MUSEUM

Address: Gablerstrasse 15, 8002 Zürich, Switzerland.

Phone: +41 44 206 31 31.

Exhibitions and collections: Rietberg Museum showcases the art and cultures of non-European countries, including Africa, Asia, Oceania, and the Americas.

Admission fees and hours of operation: Admission fees for adults are CHF 18. The museum is open from 10:00 AM to 5:00 PM from Tuesday to Sunday.

Historical background: Rietberg Museum was founded in 1952 and is the only museum in Switzerland dedicated to non-European art and cultures.

Highlights and must-sees: Some of the must-see exhibitions at Rietberg Museum include the collections of African art, Asian art, and Oceanic art.

Curiosity and facts: Rietberg Museum has one of the largest collections of non-European art in Europe.

Advice: It is recommended to allocate at least 2-3 hours to fully explore Rietberg Museum.

Getting there: Rietberg Museum is located in the heart of Zurich, within walking distance of the main railway station. From the main railway station, take the exit towards Bahnhofstrasse and walk straight ahead until you reach the museum.

Nearby attractions: Some of the nearby attractions include Bahnhofstrasse, Lake Zurich, and the Old Town.

ZURICH MUSEUM OF DESIGN

Address: Ausstellungsstrasse 60, 8005 Zürich, Switzerland.

Phone: +41 43 446 33 33.

Exhibitions and collections: Zurich Museum of Design showcases the history and evolution of design, including product design, graphic design, and architecture.

Admission fees and hours of operation: Admission fees for adults are CHF 16. The museum is open from 10:00 AM to 5:00 PM from Tuesday to Sunday.

Historical background: Zurich Museum of Design was founded in 1983 and is dedicated to the history and evolution of design in Switzerland and internationally.

Highlights and must-sees: Some of the must-see exhibitions at Zurich Museum of Design include the collections of Swiss design, product design, and graphic design.

Curiosity and facts: Zurich Museum of Design is one of the leading institutions for design in Switzerland, with a rich collection of over 40,000 objects and archives.

Advice: It is recommended to allocate at least 2-3 hours to fully explore Zurich Museum of Design.

Getting there: Zurich Museum of Design is located in the heart of Zurich, within walking distance of the main railway station. From the main railway station, take the exit towards Bahnhofstrasse and walk straight ahead until you reach the museum.

Nearby attractions: Some of the nearby attractions include Bahnhofstrasse, Lake Zurich, and the Old Town.

FIFA WORLD FOOTBALL MUSEUM

Address: Seestrasse 27, 8002 Zürich, Switzerland.

Phone: +41 44 586 00 00.

Exhibitions and collections: FIFA World Football Museum showcases the history and culture of football, including the FIFA World Cup and other major international tournaments.

Admission fees and hours of operation: Admission fees for adults are CHF 25. The museum is open from 10:00 AM to 6:00 PM from Tuesday to Sunday.

Historical background: FIFA World Football Museum was founded in 2016 and is dedicated to the history and culture of football, including the FIFA World Cup and other major international tournaments.

Highlights and must-sees: Some of the must-see exhibitions at FIFA World Football Museum include the collections of FIFA World Cup history, the Hall of Fame, and interactive exhibits on the culture of football.

Curiosity and facts: FIFA World Football Museum is the only museum in the world dedicated to the history and culture of football and is a must-visit for any football fan.

Advice: It is recommended to allocate at least 2-3 hours to fully explore FIFA World Football Museum.

Getting there: FIFA World Football Museum is located in the heart of Zurich, within walking distance of the main railway station. From the main railway station, take the exit towards Bahnhofstrasse and walk straight ahead until you reach the museum.

Nearby attractions: Some of the nearby attractions include Bahnhofstrasse, Lake Zurich, and the Old Town.

HAUS KONSTRUKTIV

Address: Selnaustrasse 25, 8001 Zürich, Switzerland.

Phone: +41 44 217 70 00.

Exhibitions and collections: Haus Konstruktiv showcases the art and culture of Constructivism, Concrete Art, and kinetic art.

Admission fees and hours of operation: Admission fees for adults are CHF 16. The museum is open from 11:00 AM to 6:00 PM from Tuesday to Sunday.

Historical background: Haus Konstruktiv was founded in 1989 and is dedicated to the art and culture of Constructivism, Concrete Art, and kinetic art.

Highlights and must-sees: Some of the must-see exhibitions at Haus Konstruktiv include the collections of Constructivist and Concrete Art, as well as kinetic art.

Curiosity and facts: Haus Konstruktiv is the only museum in Switzerland dedicated to Constructivism, Concrete Art, and kinetic art, and is a must-visit for art lovers interested in these movements.

Advice: It is recommended to allocate at least 2-3 hours to fully explore Haus Konstruktiv.

Getting there: Haus Konstruktiv is located in the heart of Zurich, within walking distance of the main railway station. From the main railway station, take the exit towards Bahnhofstrasse and walk straight ahead until you reach the museum.

Nearby attractions: Some of the nearby attractions include Bahnhofstrasse, Lake Zurich, and the Old Town.

UHRENMUSEUM BEYER

Address: Bahnhofstrasse 31, 8001 Zürich, Switzerland.

Phone: +41 44 217 70 70.

Exhibitions and collections: Uhrenmuseum Beyer showcases the history and evolution of watchmaking, including the development of timekeeping devices and the history of Swiss watchmaking.

Admission fees and hours of operation: Admission fees for adults are CHF 16. The museum is open from 10:00 AM to 6:00 PM from Tuesday to Sunday.

Historical background: Uhrenmuseum Beyer was founded in 1988 and is dedicated to the history and evolution of watchmaking, including the development of timekeeping devices and the history of Swiss watchmaking.

Highlights and must-sees: Some of the must-see exhibitions at Uhrenmuseum Beyer include the collections of antique timekeeping devices, the history of Swiss watchmaking, and the evolution of watchmaking technology.

Curiosity and facts: Uhrenmuseum Beyer is one of the leading institutions for the history of watchmaking in Switzerland and is a must-visit for anyone interested in this fascinating subject.

Advice: It is recommended to allocate at least 2-3 hours to fully explore Uhrenmuseum Beyer.

Getting there: Uhrenmuseum Beyer is located in the heart of Zurich, near the main railway station. From the main railway station, take the exit towards Bahnhofstrasse and walk straight ahead until you reach the museum.

Nearby attractions: Some of the nearby attractions include Bahnhofstrasse, Lake Zurich, and the Old Town.

ZOOLOGICAL MUSEUM

Address: Karl-Schmid-Strasse 4, 8008 Zürich, Switzerland.

Phone: +41 44 635 55 55.

Exhibitions and collections: Zoological Museum showcases the diversity of animal life, including specimens from around the world and interactive exhibits on animal behavior and ecology.

Admission fees and hours of operation: Admission fees for adults are CHF 15. The museum is open from 10:00 AM to 5:00 PM from Tuesday to Sunday.

Historical background: Zoological Museum was founded in 1847 and is one of the oldest museums of its kind in Switzerland.

Highlights and must-sees: Some of the must-see exhibitions at Zoological Museum include the collections of exotic animals, interactive exhibits on animal behavior and ecology, and the exhibitions on the evolution of life on Earth.

Curiosity and facts: Zoological Museum is home to one of the largest collections of animal specimens in Switzerland and is a must-visit for anyone interested in the diversity of animal life.

Advice: It is recommended to allocate at least 2-3 hours to fully explore Zoological Museum.

Getting there: Zoological Museum is located in the heart of Zurich, near the main railway station. From the main railway station, take the exit towards Bahnhofstrasse and walk straight ahead until you reach the museum.

Nearby attractions: Some of the nearby attractions include Bahnhofstrasse, Lake Zurich, and the Old Town.

MUSEUM FÜR GESTALTUNG

Address: Ausstellungsstrasse 60, 8005 Zürich, Switzerland.

Phone: +41 43 446 33 33.

Exhibitions and collections: Museum für Gestaltung showcases the history and evolution of design, including product design, graphic design, and architecture.

Admission fees and hours of operation: Admission fees for adults are CHF 16. The museum is open from 10:00 AM to 5:00 PM from Tuesday to Sunday.

Historical background: Museum für Gestaltung was founded in 1875 and is one of the oldest museums of its kind in Switzerland.

Highlights and must-sees: Some of the must-see exhibitions at Museum für Gestaltung include the collections of Swiss design, product design, and graphic design, as well as the exhibitions on the evolution of design and architecture.

Curiosity and facts: Museum für Gestaltung is home to one of the largest collections of design objects and archives in Switzerland and is a must-visit for anyone interested in the history and evolution of design.

Advice: It is recommended to allocate at least 2-3 hours to fully explore Museum für Gestaltung.

Getting there: Museum für Gestaltung is located in the heart of Zurich, near the main railway station. From the main railway station, take the exit towards Bahnhofstrasse and walk straight ahead until you reach the museum.

Nearby attractions: Some of the nearby attractions include Bahnhofstrasse, Lake Zurich, and the Old Town.

TRAM MUSEUM ZURICH

Address: Bahnhofstrasse 31, 8001 Zürich, Switzerland.

Phone: +41 44 217 70 00.

Exhibitions and collections: Tram Museum Zurich showcases the history and evolution of trams in Zurich, including the development of tram technology and the cultural significance of trams in the city.

Admission fees and hours of operation: Admission fees for adults are CHF 12. The museum is open from 10:00 AM to 5:00 PM from Tuesday to Sunday.

Historical background: Tram Museum Zurich was founded in 2005 and is dedicated to the history and evolution of trams in Zurich, including the development of tram technology and the cultural significance of trams in the city.

Highlights and must-sees: Some of the must-see exhibitions at Tram Museum Zurich include the collections of historic trams, interactive exhibits on tram technology, and exhibitions on the cultural significance of trams in the city.

Curiosity and facts: Tram Museum Zurich is the only museum of its kind in Switzerland and is a must-visit for anyone interested in the history and evolution of trams in Zurich.

Advice: It is recommended to allocate at least 2-3 hours to fully explore Tram Museum Zurich.

Getting there: Tram Museum Zurich is located in the heart of Zurich, near the main railway station. From the main railway station, take the exit towards Bahnhofstrasse and walk straight ahead until you reach the museum.

Nearby attractions: Some of the nearby attractions include Bahnhofstrasse, Lake Zurich, and the Old Town.

THEATERS

SCHAUSPIELHAUS ZÜRICH

Address: Schauspielhaus Zürich, Claridenstrasse 7, 8001 Zurich, Switzerland

Phone: +41 44 258 75 75

Performances and shows: The Schauspielhaus Zürich is one of the leading theaters in Switzerland, showcasing a wide range of performances, from classical plays to contemporary works.

Ticket prices and availability: Ticket prices vary depending on the performance and seat location, and can be purchased online or at the box office. Availability may vary, so it's best to check ahead of time.

Show times: Show times vary depending on the performance and can be found on the theater's website or by contacting the box office.

Historical background: The Schauspielhaus Zürich was founded in 1891 and has since established itself as one of the leading theaters in Switzerland, playing host to some of the country's most prominent actors and productions.

Highlights and must-sees: Some must-see performances at the Schauspielhaus Zürich include classical plays such as "Hamlet" and contemporary works like "Angels in America."

Curiosity and facts: The Schauspielhaus Zürich is one of the largest theaters in Switzerland, with a seating capacity of over 1000 people.

Advice: Arrive early to allow time for parking and to find your seat, and be sure to dress appropriately for the performance.

Getting there: The Schauspielhaus Zürich is located a short walk from the Paradeplatz tram station, and is easily accessible by public transportation. To get there by metro, take the number 2 or 4 to Paradeplatz and walk for 5 minutes to the theater.

Nearby attractions: Some nearby attractions include the Bahnhofstrasse shopping district, the Lake Zurich, and the Old Town.

THEATER NEUMARKT

Address: TheaterNeumarkt, Neumarkt 9, 8001 Zurich, Switzerland

Phone: +41 44 252 55 55

Performances and shows: The TheaterNeumarkt is a dynamic and versatile theater, showcasing a wide range of performances including drama, comedy, and musicals.

Ticket prices and availability: Ticket prices vary depending on the performance and seat location, and can be purchased online or at the box office. Availability may vary, so it's best to check ahead of time.

Show times: Show times vary depending on the performance and can be found on the theater's website or by contacting the box office.

Historical background: The TheaterNeumarkt was established in the 19th century and has since been a prominent cultural center in Zurich, showcasing a diverse range of performances and productions.

Highlights and must-sees: Some must-see performances at the TheaterNeumarkt include classical plays such as

"A Midsummer Night's Dream" and contemporary works like "The Importance of Being Earnest."

Curiosity and facts: The TheaterNeumarkt is known for its beautiful architecture and acoustics, making it a popular venue for musical performances and concerts.

Advice: Arrive early to allow time for parking and to find your seat, and be sure to dress appropriately for the performance.

Getting there: The TheaterNeumarkt is located a short walk from the St. Annahof tram station, and is easily accessible by public transportation. To get there by metro, take the number 2 or 4 to St. Annahof and walk for 5 minutes to the theater.

Nearby attractions: Some nearby attractions include the Bahnhofstrasse shopping district, the Lake Zurich, and the Old Town.

THEATER AM HECHTPLATZ

Address: Theater am Hechtplatz, Hechtplatz 5, 8008 Zurich, Switzerland

Phone: +41 44 201 68 68

Performances and shows: The Theater am Hechtplatz is a dynamic and versatile theater, showcasing a wide range of performances including drama, comedy, and musicals.

Ticket prices and availability: Ticket prices vary depending on the performance and seat location, and can be purchased online or at the box office. Availability may vary, so it's best to check ahead of time.

Show times: Show times vary depending on the performance and can be found on the theater's website or by contacting the box office.

Historical background: The Theater am Hechtplatz was established in the early 20th century and has since been a prominent cultural center in Zurich, showcasing a diverse range of performances and productions.

Highlights and must-sees: Some must-see performances at the Theater am Hechtplatz include classical plays such as "Romeo and Juliet" and contemporary works like "The Laramie Project."

Curiosity and facts: The Theater am Hechtplatz is known for its innovative productions and use of modern technology in its performances.

Advice: Arrive early to allow time for parking and to find your seat, and be sure to dress appropriately for the performance.

Getting there: The Theater am Hechtplatz is located a short walk from the Stauffacher tram station, and is easily accessible by public transportation. To get there by metro, take the number 2 or 4 to Stauffacher and walk for 5 minutes to the theater.

Nearby attractions: Some nearby attractions include the Bahnhofstrasse shopping district, the Lake Zurich, and the Old Town.

MILLERS

Address: Millers, Neumühlequai 55, 8006 Zurich, Switzerland

Phone: +41 44 201 68 68

Performances and shows: Millers is a modern theater and cultural center, showcasing a wide range of performances including theater, dance, and live music.

Ticket prices and availability: Ticket prices vary depending on the performance and seat location, and can be purchased online or at the box office. Availability may vary, so it's best to check ahead of time.

Show times: Show times vary depending on the performance and can be found on the theater's website or by contacting the box office.

Historical background: Millers was established in the late 20th century and has since become one of the most innovative and dynamic cultural centers in Zurich, showcasing a diverse range of performances and events.

Highlights and must-sees: Some must-see performances at Millers include experimental theater productions and innovative dance performances.

Curiosity and facts: Millers is known for its unique and modern design, and its commitment to promoting cutting-edge and innovative art and culture.

Advice: Arrive early to allow time for parking and to find your seat, and be sure to dress appropriately for the performance.

Getting there: Millers is located a short walk from the Tiefenbrunnen tram station, and is easily accessible by public transportation. To get there by metro, take the number 2 or 4 to Tiefenbrunnen and walk for 5 minutes to the theater.

Nearby attractions: Some nearby attractions include the Bahnhofstrasse shopping district, the Lake Zurich, and the Old Town.

THEATER RIGIBLICK

Address: TheaterRigiblick, Zollikerstrasse 121, 8050 Zurich, Switzerland

Phone: +41 43 443 11 11

Performances and shows: The TheaterRigiblick is a community theater, showcasing a wide range of performances including theater, dance, and live music.

Ticket prices and availability: Ticket prices vary depending on the performance and seat location, and can be purchased online or at the box office. Availability may vary, so it's best to check ahead of time.

Show times: Show times vary depending on the performance and can be found on the theater's website or by contacting the box office.

Historical background: The TheaterRigiblick was established in the mid 20th century as a community theater, and has since been a cultural hub for the local community, showcasing a diverse range of performances and events.

Highlights and must-sees: Some must-see performances at the TheaterRigiblick include locally produced plays and musicals, as well as community events and workshops.

Curiosity and facts: The TheaterRigiblick is known for its strong community spirit and commitment to promoting local talent and art.

Advice: Arrive early to allow time for parking and to find your seat, and be sure to dress appropriately for the performance.

Getting there: The TheaterRigiblick is located a short walk from the Oerlikon tram station, and is easily accessible by public transportation. To get there by metro, take the number 2 or 4 to Oerlikon and walk for 5 minutes to the theater.

Nearby attractions: Some nearby attractions include the Bahnhofstrasse shopping district, the Lake Zurich, and the Old Town.

GESSNERALLEE

Address: Gessnerallee, Limmatstrasse 118, 8005 Zurich, Switzerland

Phone: +41 43 443 11 11

Performances and shows: Gessnerallee is a cutting-edge theater and cultural center, showcasing a wide range of performances including theater, dance, and live music.

Ticket prices and availability: Ticket prices vary depending on the performance and seat location, and can be purchased online or at the box office. Availability may vary, so it's best to check ahead of time.

Show times: Show times vary depending on the performance and can be found on the theater's website or by contacting the box office.

Historical background: Gessnerallee was established in the late 20th century as a center for innovative and cutting-edge art and culture, and has since been a leading cultural venue in Zurich.

Highlights and must-sees: Some must-see performances at Gessnerallee include experimental theater productions and innovative dance performances.

Curiosity and facts: Gessnerallee is known for its commitment to promoting and supporting cutting-edge and avant-garde art and culture.

Advice: Arrive early to allow time for parking and to find your seat, and be sure to dress appropriately for the performance.

Getting there: Gessnerallee is located a short walk from the Hardbrücke tram station, and is easily accessible by public transportation. To get there by metro, take the number 2 or 4 to Hardbrücke and walk for 5 minutes to the theater.

Nearby attractions: Some nearby attractions include the Bahnhofstrasse shopping district, the Lake Zurich, and the Old Town.

MAAG HALLE

Address: Maag Halle, Limmatstrasse 270, 8005 Zurich, Switzerland

Phone: +41 43 443 11 11

Performances and shows: Maag Halle is a versatile and dynamic cultural center, showcasing a wide range of performances including theater, dance, and live music.

Ticket prices and availability: Ticket prices vary depending on the performance and seat location, and can be purchased online or at the box office. Availability may vary, so it's best to check ahead of time.

Show times: Show times vary depending on the performance and can be found on the theater's website or by contacting the box office.

Historical background: Maag Halle was established in the late 20th century as a cultural hub for the local community, and has since been a leading venue for cultural events and performances in Zurich.

Highlights and must-sees: Some must-see performances at Maag Halle include locally produced plays and musicals, as well as live music concerts and cultural events.

Curiosity and facts: Maag Halle is known for its vibrant and dynamic cultural scene, and its commitment to promoting local talent and art.

Advice: Arrive early to allow time for parking and to find your seat, and be sure to dress appropriately for the performance.

Getting there: Maag Halle is located a short walk from the Hardbrücke tram station, and is easily accessible by public transportation. To get there by metro, take the number 2 or 4 to Hardbrücke and walk for 5 minutes to the theater.

Nearby attractions: Some nearby attractions include the Bahnhofstrasse shopping district, the Lake Zurich, and the Old Town.

THEATER STOK

Address: Theater Stok, Sihlquai 240, 8005 Zurich, Switzerland

Phone: +41 43 443 11 11

Performances and shows: Theater Stok is a modern and dynamic cultural center, showcasing a wide range of performances including theater, dance, and live music.

Ticket prices and availability: Ticket prices vary depending on the performance and seat location, and can be purchased online or at the box office. Availability may vary, so it's best to check ahead of time.

Show times: Show times vary depending on the performance and can be found on the theater's website or by contacting the box office.

Historical background: Theater Stok was established in the late 20th century as a center for innovative and cutting-edge art and culture, and has since been a leading cultural venue in Zurich.

Highlights and must-sees: Some must-see performances at Theater Stok include experimental theater productions and innovative dance performances.

Curiosity and facts: Theater Stok is known for its commitment to promoting and supporting cutting-edge and avant-garde art and culture.

Advice: Arrive early to allow time for parking and to find your seat, and be sure to dress appropriately for the performance.

Getting there: Theater Stok is located a short walk from the Hardbrücke tram station, and is easily accessible by public transportation. To get there by metro, take the number 2 or 4 to Hardbrücke and walk for 5 minutes to the theater.

Nearby attractions: Some nearby attractions include the Bahnhofstrasse shopping district, the Lake Zurich, and the Old Town.

CABARET VOLTAIRE

Address: Cabaret Voltaire, Spiegelgasse 1, 8001 Zurich, Switzerland

Phone: +41 43 443 11 11

Performances and shows: Cabaret Voltaire is a historic and iconic cultural center, showcasing a wide range of performances including theater, dance, and live music.

Ticket prices and availability: Ticket prices vary depending on the performance and seat location, and can be purchased online or at the box office. Availability may vary, so it's best to check ahead of time.

Show times: Show times vary depending on the performance and can be found on the theater's website or by contacting the box office.

Historical background: Cabaret Voltaire was established in 1916 as a center for avant-garde art and culture, and is considered one of the birthplace of the Dada movement. Today, it continues to be a leading cultural venue in Zurich.

Highlights and must-sees: Some must-see performances at Cabaret Voltaire include experimental theaterproductions and innovative dance performances, as well as live music concerts and cultural events.

Curiosity and facts: Cabaret Voltaire is known for its rich history and association with the Dada movement, and its commitment to promoting and supporting avant-garde and experimental art and culture.

Advice: Arrive early to allow time for parking and to find your seat, and be sure to dress appropriately for the performance.

Getting there: Cabaret Voltaire is located a short walk from the Central tram station, and is easily accessible by public transportation. To get there by metro, take the number 2 or 4 to Central and walk for 5 minutes to the theater.

Nearby attractions: Some nearby attractions include the Bahnhofstrasse shopping district, the Lake Zurich, and the Old Town.

CASINOTHEATER WINTERTHUR

Address: Casinotheater Winterthur, Bahnhofstrasse 56, 8400 Winterthur, Switzerland

Phone: +41 52 267 71 71

Performances and shows: Casinotheater Winterthur is a modern and dynamic cultural center, showcasing a wide range of performances including theater, dance, and live music.

Ticket prices and availability: Ticket prices vary depending on the performance and seat location, and can be purchased online or at the box office. Availability may vary, so it's best to check ahead of time.

Show times: Show times vary depending on the performance and can be found on the theater's website or by contacting the box office.

Historical background: Casinotheater Winterthur was established in the late 20th century as a cultural hub for the local community, and has since been a leading venue for cultural events and performances in Winterthur.

Highlights and must-sees: Some must-see performances at Casinotheater Winterthur include locally produced plays and musicals, as well as live music concerts and cultural events.

Curiosity and facts: Casinotheater Winterthur is known for its vibrant and dynamic cultural scene, and its commitment to promoting local talent and art.

Advice: Arrive early to allow time for parking and to find your seat, and be sure to dress appropriately for the performance.

Getting there: Casinotheater Winterthur is located a short walk from the Winterthur train station, and is easily accessible by public transportation. To get there by train, take the number 2 or 4 to Winterthur and walk for 5 minutes to the theater.

Nearby attractions: Some nearby attractions include the Bahnhofstrasse shopping district, the Lake Zurich, and the Old Town of Winterthur.

GALLERIES

GALERIE HAUSER & WIRTH

Address: Limmatstrasse 270, 8005 Zurich, Switzerland.

Phone: +41 44 446 80 50.

Exhibitions and collections: The gallery is known for its exhibitions of contemporary and modern art, including works by Pablo Picasso, Joan Miró, and Paul Klee.

Admission fees and hours of operation: Admission is free, and the gallery is open from Tuesday to Friday from 11 am to 6 pm and on weekends from 10 am to 5 pm.

Historical background: Galerie Hauser & Wirth was established in 1992 by Iwan and Manuela Wirth and Ursula Hauser in Switzerland. The gallery has since expanded to multiple locations worldwide.

Highlights and must-sees: Some of the must-see exhibitions at the gallery include solo shows by contemporary artists such as Mark Bradford and Paul McCarthy.

Curiosity and facts: The gallery also operates a contemporary art bookstore and a restaurant, making it a hub for art lovers in Zurich.

Advice: Plan your visit in advance to ensure that you can see all of the exhibitions that interest you, and consider visiting the restaurant for a bite to eat after your visit.

Getting there: The gallery is a short walk from the Hardbrücke tram and train station. Take tram no. 2 or 4 to the "Waffenplatzstrasse" stop, and walk for about five minutes to reach the gallery.

Nearby attractions: Some nearby attractions include the Swiss National Museum and the Kunsthaus Zurich.

GALERIE BOB GYSIN

Address: Talstrasse 83, 8001 Zurich, Switzerland.

Phone: +41 44 251 55 55.

Exhibitions and collections: Galerie Bob Gysin specializes in contemporary art, with a focus on Swiss and international artists.

Admission fees and hours of operation: Admission is free, and the gallery is open from Tuesday to Friday from 11 am to 6 pm and on weekends from 11 am to 5 pm.

Historical background: The gallery was founded in 2000 by Bob Gysin and is located in the heart of Zurich's art district.

Highlights and must-sees: Some of the must-see exhibitions at the gallery include solo shows by emerging Swiss artists and group exhibitions featuring works by contemporary artists from around the world.

Curiosity and facts: The gallery also offers private art consulting services, helping clients build their personal art collections.

Advice: Plan your visit in advance to ensure that you can see all of the exhibitions that interest you, and consider reaching out to the gallery for private art consulting services if you are looking to build your personal art collection.

Getting there: The gallery is located a short walk from the Paradeplatz tram and train station. Take tram no. 2, 4, or 13 to the "Paradeplatz" stop, and walk for about five minutes to reach the gallery.

Nearby attractions: Some nearby attractions include the Bahnhofstrasse shopping street and the Zurich Opera House.

GALERIE KERNWEINE

Address: Limmatstrasse 270, 8005 Zurich, Switzerland.

Phone: +41 44 446 80 60.

Exhibitions and collections: Galerie Kernweine is known for its exhibitions of contemporary art, with a focus on Swiss and international artists.

Admission fees and hours of operation: Admission is free, and the gallery is open from Tuesday to Friday from 11 am to 6 pm and on weekends from 11 am to 5 pm.

Historical background: The gallery was established in 1990 and is located in the heart of Zurich's art district.

Highlights and must-sees: Some of the must-see exhibitions at the gallery include solo shows by contemporary Swiss artists and group exhibitions featuring works by international artists.

Curiosity and facts: The gallery also offers private art consulting services, helping clients build their personal art collections.

Advice: Plan your visit in advance to ensure that you can see all of the exhibitions that interest you, and consider reaching out to the gallery for private art consulting services if you are looking to build your personal art collection.

Getting there: The gallery is located a short walk from the Hardbrücke tram and train station. Take tram no. 2 or 4 to the "Waffenplatzstrasse" stop, and walk for about five minutes to reach the gallery.

Nearby attractions: Some nearby attractions include the Swiss National Museum and the Kunsthaus Zurich.

GALERIE PETER KILCHMANN

Address: Limmatstrasse 270, 8005 Zurich, Switzerland.

Phone: +41 44 272 15 15.

Exhibitions and collections: Galerie Peter Kilchmann is known for its exhibitions of contemporary art, with a focus on Swiss and international artists.

Admission fees and hours of operation: Admission is free, and the gallery is open from Tuesday to Friday from 11 am to 6 pm and on weekends from 11 am to 5 pm.

Historical background: The gallery was established in 1995 and is located in the heart of Zurich's art district.

Highlights and must-sees: Some of the must-see exhibitions at the gallery include solo shows by contemporary Swiss artists and group exhibitions featuring works by international artists.

Curiosity and facts: The gallery also offers private art consulting services, helping clients build their personal art collections.

Advice: Plan your visit in advance to ensure that you can see all of the exhibitions that interest you, and consider reaching out to the gallery for private art consulting services if you are looking to build your personal art collection.

Getting there: The gallery is located a short walk from the Hardbrücke tram and train station. Take tram no. 2 or 4 to the "Waffenplatzstrasse" stop, and walk for about five minutes to reach the gallery.

Nearby attractions: Some nearby attractions include the Swiss National Museum and the Kunsthaus Zurich.

GALERIE CARZANIGA

Address: Limmatstrasse 270, 8005 Zurich, Switzerland.

Phone: +41 44 448 11 11.

Exhibitions and collections: Galerie Carzaniga is known for its exhibitions of contemporary art, with a focus on Swiss and international artists.

Admission fees and hours of operation: Admission is free, and the gallery is open from Tuesday to Friday from 11 am to 6 pm and on weekends from 11 am to 5 pm.

Historical background: The gallery was established in 1990 and is located in the heart of Zurich's art district.

Highlights and must-sees: Some of the must-see exhibitions at the gallery include solo shows by contemporary Swiss artists and group exhibitions featuring works by international artists.

Curiosity and facts: The gallery also offers private art consulting services, helping clients build their personal art collections.

Advice: Plan your visit in advance to ensure that you can see all of the exhibitions that interest you, and consider reaching out to the gallery for private art consulting services if you are looking to build your personal art collection.

Getting there: The gallery is located a short walk from the Hardbrücke tram and train station. Take tram no. 2 or 4 to the "Waffenplatzstrasse" stop, and walk for about five minutes to reach the gallery.

Nearby attractions: Some nearby attractions include the Swiss National Museum and the Kunsthaus Zurich.

GALERIE GMURZYNSKA

Address: Talstrasse 83, 8001 Zurich, Switzerland.

Phone: +41 44 251 55 50.

Exhibitions and collections: Galerie Gmurzynska specializes in modern and contemporary art, with a focus on works by 20th-century artists.

Admission fees and hours of operation: Admission is free, and the gallery is open from Tuesday to Friday from 11 am to 6 pm and on weekends from 11 am to 5 pm.

Historical background: The gallery was founded in 1965 and has since become one of the leading galleries for modern and contemporary art in Europe.

Highlights and must-sees: Some of the must-see exhibitions at the gallery include solo shows by modern artists such as Pablo Picasso and Joan Miró, as well as group exhibitions featuring works by contemporary artists.

Curiosity and facts: Galerie Gmurzynska has played a significant role in the development of the contemporary art market and has organized some of the most important exhibitions of modern and contemporary art in Europe.

Advice: Plan your visit in advance to ensure that you can see all of the exhibitions that interest you, and take your time to appreciate the works on display.

Getting there: The gallery is located a short walk from the Paradeplatz tram and train station. Take tram no. 2, 4, or 13 to the "Paradeplatz" stop, and walk for about five minutes to reach the gallery.

Nearby attractions: Some nearby attractions include the Bahnhofstrasse shopping street and the Zurich Opera House.

LÖWENBRÄU ART COMPLEX

Address: Limmatstrasse 270, 8005 Zurich, Switzerland.

Phone: +41 44 446 80 40.

Exhibitions and collections: The Löwenbräu Art Complex is a multi-disciplinary arts center, with exhibitions and events in the fields of visual arts, performance, and music.

Admission fees and hours of operation: Admission fees vary based on the exhibition or event, and hours of operation vary based on the schedule. Check the website for up-to-date information.

Historical background: The Löwenbräu Art Complex was established in the early 20th century and has since become a hub for contemporary and modern art in Zurich.

Highlights and must-sees: Some of the must-see exhibitions and events at the complex include solo shows by contemporary artists and experimental performance pieces.

Curiosity and facts: The complex is housed in a historic building that was once a brewery, adding to its unique and eclectic atmosphere.

Advice: Plan your visit in advance to ensure that you can see all of the exhibitions and events that interest you, and consider checking out the surrounding neighborhood for additional cultural experiences.

Getting there: The Löwenbräu Art Complex is located a short walk from the Hardbrücke tram and train station. Take tram no. 2 or 4 to the "Waffenplatzstrasse" stop, and walk for about five minutes to reach the complex.

Nearby attractions: Some nearby attractions include the Swiss National Museum and the Kunsthaus Zurich.

GALERIE EVA PRESENHUBER

Address: Zürcherstrasse 158, 8005 Zurich, Switzerland.

Phone: +41 44 446 80 50.

Exhibitions and collections: Galerie Eva Presenhuber specializes in contemporary art, with a focus on works by international artists.

Admission fees and hours of operation: Admission is free, and the gallery is open from Tuesday to Friday from 11 am to 6 pm and on weekends from 11 am to 5 pm.

Historical background: The gallery was established in 1990 and is located in the heart of Zurich's art district.

Highlights and must-sees: Some of the must-see exhibitions at the gallery include solo shows by contemporary international artists and group exhibitions featuring works by up-and-coming artists.

Curiosity and facts: The gallery also offers private art consulting services, helping clients build their personal art collections.

Advice: Plan your visit in advance to ensure that you can see all of the exhibitions that interest you, and consider reaching out to the gallery for private art consulting services if you are looking to build your personal art collection.

Getting there: The gallery is located a short walk from the Hardbrücke tram and train station. Take tram no. 2 or 4 to the "Waffenplatzstrasse" stop, and walk for about five minutes to reach the gallery.

Nearby attractions: Some nearby attractions include the Swiss National Museum and the Kunsthaus Zurich.

GALERIE MEILE

Address: Meilenstrasse 54, 8002 Zurich, Switzerland.

Phone: +41 44 251 51 51.

Exhibitions and collections: Galerie Meile specializes in contemporary art, with a focus on works by Swiss and international artists.

Admission fees and hours of operation: Admission is free, and the gallery is open from Tuesday to Friday from 11 am to 6 pm and on weekends from 11 am to 5 pm.

Historical background: The gallery was established in 1990 and is located in the heart of Zurich's art district.

Highlights and must-sees: Some of the must-see exhibitions at the gallery include solo shows by contemporary Swiss and international artists and group exhibitions featuring works by up-and-coming artists.

Curiosity and facts: The gallery also offers private art consulting services, helping clients build their personal art collections.

Advice: Plan your visit in advance to ensure that you can see all of the exhibitions that interest you, and consider reaching out to the gallery for private art consulting services if you are looking to build your personal art collection.

Getting there: The gallery is located a short walk from the Paradeplatz tram and train station. Take tram no. 2, 4, or 13 to the "Paradeplatz" stop, and walk for about five minutes to reach the gallery.

Nearby attractions: Some nearby attractions include the Bahnhofstrasse shopping street and the Zurich Opera House.

GALERIE MAI 36

Address: Röntgenstrasse 1, 8005 Zurich, Switzerland.

Phone: +41 44 252 38 80.

Exhibitions and collections: Galerie Mai 36 specializes in contemporary art, with a focus on works by Swiss and international artists.

Admission fees and hours of operation: Admission is free, and the gallery is open from Tuesday to Friday from 11 am to 6 pm and on weekends from 11 am to 5 pm.

Historical background: The gallery was established in 1986 and is located in the heart of Zurich's art district.

Highlights and must-sees: Some of the must-see exhibitions at the gallery include solo shows by contemporary Swiss and international artists and group exhibitions featuring works by up-and-coming artists.

Curiosity and facts: The gallery also offers private art consulting services, helping clients build their personal art collections.

Advice: Plan your visit in advance to ensure that you can see all of the exhibitions that interest you, and consider reaching out to the gallery for private art consulting services if you are looking to build your personal art collection.

Getting there: The gallery is located a short walk from the Hardbrücke tram and train station. Take tram no. 2 or 4 to the "Waffenplatzstrasse" stop, and walk for about five minutes to reach the gallery.

Nearby attractions: Some nearby attractions include the Swiss National Museum and the Kunsthaus Zurich.

TOURS

ZURICH TUK TUK TOUR

Address: 123 Main Street, Zurich, Switzerland

Phone: +41 123 456 789

Itinerary and highlights: Explore the city of Zurich in a unique and fun way on a TukTuk tour. Visit some of the most famous landmarks and hidden gems of the city. Experience the local culture and history. Enjoy stunning views of the city and its surroundings.

Tour length and cost: 2 hours, CHF 100 per person

Tour guide and language options: English and German speaking guides available

Meeting location and transportation: Meet at the TukTuk station located at Bahnhofstrasse, Zurich. Transportation by TukTuk included in the tour price.

Historical background: Learn about the history of Zurich and its evolution from a Roman settlement to a modern financial center.

Highlights and must-sees: Visit the picturesque old town, the famous Bahnhofstrasse shopping street, the scenic Lake Zurich, and the beautiful Grossmünster church.

Curiosity and facts: Discover the fascinating facts and stories behind the city and its landmarks.

Advice: Wear comfortable shoes and bring a camera to capture the beautiful sights.

Getting there: Take the metro to Bahnhofstrasse station and walk to the TukTuk station located nearby.

Nearby attractions: Visit the Swiss National Museum, the Uetliberg Mountain, and the Zurich Zoo.

OLD TOWN WALKING TOUR

Address: 123 Main Street, Zurich, Switzerland

Phone: +41 123 456 789

Itinerary and highlights: Take a journey through the charming streets of the old town and discover the history and culture of Zurich. Visit some of the most famous landmarks and hidden gems of the city.

Tour length and cost: 2 hours, CHF 50 per person

Tour guide and language options: English and German speaking guides available

Meeting location and transportation: Meet at the old town entrance located at Bahnhofstrasse, Zurich. Transportation not included in the tour price.

Historical background: Learn about the history of Zurich and its evolution from a Roman settlement to a modern financial center.

Highlights and must-sees: Visit the picturesque old town, the famous Bahnhofstrasse shopping street, the scenic Lake Zurich, and the beautiful Grossmünster church.

Curiosity and facts: Discover the fascinating facts and stories behind the city and its landmarks.

Advice: Wear comfortable shoes and bring a camera to capture the beautiful sights.

Getting there: Take the metro to Bahnhofstrasse station and walk to the old town entrance located nearby.

Nearby attractions: Visit the Swiss National Museum, the Uetliberg Mountain, and the Zurich Zoo.

ZURICH BIKE TOUR

Address: 123 Main Street, Zurich, Switzerland

Phone: +41 123 456 789

Itinerary and highlights: Discover the beauty of Zurich on a bike tour. Visit some of the most famous landmarks and hidden gems of the city. Experience the local culture and history. Enjoy stunning views of the city and its surroundings.

Tour length and cost: 4 hours, CHF 80 per person

Tour guide and language options: English and German speaking guides available

Meeting location and transportation: Meet at the bike rental shop located at Bahnhofstrasse, Zurich. Transportation by bike included in the tour price.

Historical background: Learn about the history of Zurich and its evolution from a Roman settlement to a modern financial center.

Highlights and must-sees: Visit the picturesque old town, the famous Bahnhofstrasse shopping street, the scenic Lake Zurich, and the beautiful Grossmünster church.

Curiosity and facts: Discover the fascinating facts and stories behind the city and its landmarks.

Advice: Wear comfortable shoes and bring a camera to capture the beautiful sights. Bring a water bottle.

Getting there: Take the metro to Bahnhofstrasse station and walk to the bike rental shop located nearby.

Nearby attractions: Visit the Swiss National Museum, the Uetliberg Mountain, and the Zurich Zoo.

LAKE ZURICH BOAT CRUISE

Address: 123 Main Street, Zurich, Switzerland

Phone: +41 123 456 789

Itinerary and highlights: Enjoy a relaxing boat cruise on Lake Zurich. Admire the stunning views of the city and its surroundings. Learn about the history and culture of Zurich and its landmarks.

Tour length and cost: 2 hours, CHF 60 per person

Tour guide and language options: English and German speaking guides available

Meeting location and transportation: Meet at the boat dock located at Lake Zurich, Zurich. Transportation to the boat dock not included in the tour price.

Historical background: Learn about the history of Lake Zurich and its significance to the city and its residents.

Highlights and must-sees: Admire the stunning views of the city and its landmarks such as the Grossmünster church, the Uetliberg Mountain, and the Swiss National Museum.

Curiosity and facts: Discover the fascinating facts and stories about the lake and its surroundings.

Advice: Wear comfortable clothes and bring a camera to capture the beautiful sights. Bring a jacket as it can get chilly on the boat.

Getting there: Take the metro to Lake Zurich station and walk to the boat dock located nearby.

Nearby attractions: Visit the Swiss National Museum, the Uetliberg Mountain, and the Zurich Zoo.

ZURICH SEGWAY TOUR

Address: 123 Main Street, Zurich, Switzerland

Phone: +41 123 456 789

Itinerary and highlights: Explore the city of Zurich in a unique and fun way on a Segway tour. Visit some of the most famous landmarks and hidden gems of the city. Experience the local culture and history. Enjoy stunning views of the city and its surroundings.

Tour length and cost: 2 hours, CHF 90 per person

Tour guide and language options: English and German speaking guides available

Meeting location and transportation: Meet at the Segway station located at Bahnhofstrasse, Zurich. Transportation by Segway included in the tour price.

Historical background: Learn about the history of Zurich and its evolution from a Roman settlement to a modern financial center.

Highlights and must-sees: Visit the picturesque old town, the famous Bahnhofstrasse shopping street, the scenic Lake Zurich, and the beautiful Grossmünster church.

Curiosity and facts: Discover the fascinating facts and stories behind the city and its landmarks.

Advice: Wear comfortable shoes and bring a camera to capture the beautiful sights.

Getting there: Take the metro to Bahnhofstrasse station and walk to the Segway station located nearby.

Nearby attractions: Visit the Swiss National Museum, the Uetliberg Mountain, and the Zurich Zoo.

FREE WALKING TOUR ZURICH

Address: 123 Main Street, Zurich, Switzerland

Phone: +41 123 456 789

Itinerary and highlights: Join a free walking tour of Zurich and discover the city's history and culture. Visit some of the most famous landmarks and hidden gems of the city. Experience the local atmosphere and learn about Zurich's past and present.

Tour length and cost: 2 hours, free of charge (tips for the guide are appreciated)

Tour guide and language options: English and German speaking guides available

Meeting location and transportation: Meet at the designated meeting point located at Bahnhofstrasse, Zurich. Transportation not included in the tour price.

Historical background: Learn about the history of Zurich and its evolution from a Roman settlement to a modern financial center.

Highlights and must-sees: Visit the picturesque old town, the famous Bahnhofstrasse shopping street, the scenic Lake Zurich, and the beautiful Grossmünster church.

Curiosity and facts: Discover the fascinating facts and stories behind the city and its landmarks.

Advice: Wear comfortable shoes and bring a camera to capture the beautiful sights.

Getting there: Take the metro to Bahnhofstrasse station and walk to the designated meeting point located nearby.

Nearby attractions: Visit the Swiss National Museum, the Uetliberg Mountain, and the Zurich Zoo.

ZURICH FOOD TOUR

Address: 123 Main Street, Zurich, Switzerland

Phone: +41 123 456 789

Itinerary and highlights: Join a food tour of Zurich and taste the local cuisine. Discover the city's food culture and learn about the history and traditions behind the dishes. Visit some of the best restaurants and cafes in Zurich.

Tour length and cost: 3 hours, CHF 120 per person

Tour guide and language options: English and German speaking guides available

Meeting location and transportation: Meet at the designated meeting point located at Bahnhofstrasse, Zurich. Transportation not included in the tour price.

Historical background: Learn about the history of Zurich's food culture and its evolution over time.

Highlights and must-tastes: Taste traditional Swiss dishes such as Raclette and Rösti, and local specialties such as chocolate and cheese.

Curiosity and facts: Discover the fascinating facts and stories behind the city's food and its dishes.

Advice: Come with an empty stomach and an open mind for new culinary experiences.

Getting there: Take the metro to Bahnhofstrasse station and walk to the designated meeting point located nearby.

Nearby attractions: Visit the Swiss National Museum, the Uetliberg Mountain, and the Zurich Zoo.

E-BIKE WINE TOUR

Address: 123 Main Street, Zurich, Switzerland

Phone: +41 123 456 789

Itinerary and highlights: Join a wine tour of Zurich on an e-bike. Discover the local wine culture and visit some of the best vineyards in the area. Taste various types of wine and learn about the history and traditions behind the wine-making process.

Tour length and cost: 4 hours, CHF 150 per person

Tour guide and language options: English and German speaking guides available

Meeting location and transportation: Meet at the e-bike rental shop located at Bahnhofstrasse, Zurich. Transportation by e-bike included in the tour price.

Historical background: Learn about the history of Zurich's wine culture and its evolution over time.

Highlights and must-tastes: Taste various types of wine from the local vineyards and learn about the wine-making process.

Curiosity and facts: Discover the fascinating facts and stories behind the local wine culture and its wines.

Advice: Come with an open mind for new wine experiences and be prepared to taste some delicious wines.

Getting there: Take the metro to Bahnhofstrasse station and walk to the e-bike rental shop located nearby.

Nearby attractions: Visit the Swiss National Museum, the Uetliberg Mountain, and the Zurich Zoo.

ZURICH CHOCOLATE TOUR

Address: 123 Main Street, Zurich, Switzerland

Phone: +41 123 456 789

Itinerary and highlights: Join a chocolate tour of Zurich and discover the city's rich chocolate culture. Visit some of the best chocolate shops and factories in the city. Taste various types of chocolate and learn about the history and traditions behind chocolate-making in Zurich.

Tour length and cost: 2 hours, CHF 100 per person

Tour guide and language options: English and German speaking guides available

Meeting location and transportation: Meet at the designated meeting point located at Bahnhofstrasse, Zurich. Transportation not included in the tour price.

Historical background: Learn about the history of Zurich's chocolate culture and its evolution over time.

Highlights and must-tastes: Taste various types of chocolate from the local chocolate shops and learn about the chocolate-making process.

Curiosity and facts: Discover the fascinating facts and stories behind the local chocolate culture and its chocolates.

Advice: Come with a sweet tooth and an open mind for new chocolate experiences.

Getting there: Take the metro to Bahnhofstrasse station and walk to the designated meeting point located nearby.

Nearby attractions: Visit the Swiss National Museum, the Uetliberg Mountain, and the Zurich Zoo.

ZURICH WEST ART AND FOOD TOUR

Address: 123 Main Street, Zurich, Switzerland

Phone: +41 123 456 789

Itinerary and highlights: Join a unique tour of Zurich's West side and discover the city's art and food culture. Visit some of the best art galleries and restaurants in the area. Taste the local cuisine and learn about the history and traditions behind the dishes. Experience the local atmosphere and culture.

Tour length and cost: 4 hours, CHF 140 per person

Tour guide and language options: English and German speaking guides available

Meeting location and transportation: Meet at the designated meeting point located at Bahnhofstrasse, Zurich. Transportation not included in the tour price.

Historical background: Learn about the history of Zurich's West side and its evolution as an art and food hub.

Highlights and must-tastes: Visit the best art galleries and restaurants in the area and taste the local cuisine.

Curiosity and facts: Discover the fascinating facts and stories behind the local art and food culture.

Advice: Come with an open mind for new cultural experiences and be prepared to taste some delicious food.

Getting there: Take the metro to Bahnhofstrasse station and walk to the designated meeting point located nearby.

Nearby attractions: Visit the Swiss National Museum, the Uetliberg Mountain, and the Zurich Zoo.

WALKS

LIMMAT RIVER WALK

Address: Limmatstrasse, 8005 Zurich, Switzerland.

Phone: +41 44 267 71 71.

Route and highlights: The Limmat River Walk is a scenic walk along the Limmat River, starting from the Bahnhofstrasse and ending at the Lake Zurich. The route includes stops at the Grossmünster Church, the Fraumünster Church, and the Lindenhof Park.

Walk length and cost: The Limmat River Walk is approximately 4 kilometers long and is free of charge.

Meeting location and transportation: Meet at the Bahnhofstrasse, which can be reached by taking the tram number 2 or 4 to the Paradeplatz stop.

Historical background: The Limmat River has been a central part of Zurich's history since its founding as a Roman settlement in the 1st century AD. The river has played a key role in the city's development as a center for trade and commerce.

Highlights and must-sees: The Grossmünster Church, the Fraumünster Church, and the Lindenhof Park are all must-sees along the Limmat River Walk.

Curiosity and facts: The Limmat River is one of the major rivers in Switzerland and is an important source of drinking water for the city of Zurich.

Advice: Wear comfortable shoes and bring a hat and sunscreen if it is a sunny day.

Getting there: To reach the Bahnhofstrasse, take the tram number 2 or 4 to the Paradeplatz stop.

Nearby attractions: The Bahnhofstrasse, the Paradeplatz, and the Lake Zurich are all nearby attractions that can be easily accessed from the Limmat River Walk.

ZURICH OLD TOWN WALK

Address: Old Town, 8001 Zurich, Switzerland.

Phone: +41 44 215 40 00.

Route and highlights: The Zurich Old Town Walk is a scenic walk through the historic heart of Zurich, starting at the Bahnhofstrasse and ending at the Lake Zurich. The route includes stops at the St. Peter's Church, the Lindenhof Park, and the Fraumünster Church.

Walk length and cost: The Zurich Old Town Walk is approximately 4 kilometers long and is free of charge.

Meeting location and transportation: Meet at the Bahnhofstrasse, which can be reached by taking the tram number 2 or 4 to the Paradeplatz stop.

Historical background: The Old Town of Zurich has a rich history, dating back to the Roman era. It has been a center of trade and commerce for centuries and is home to many historic buildings and landmarks.

Highlights and must-sees: The St. Peter's Church, the Lindenhof Park, and the Fraumünster Church are all must-sees along the Zurich Old Town Walk.

Curiosity and facts: St. Peter's Church is the oldest church in Zurich and is known for its historic clock tower and stunning stained glass windows.

Advice: Wear comfortable shoes and bring a hat and sunscreen if it is a sunny day.

Getting there: To reach the Bahnhofstrasse, take the tram number 2 or 4 to the Paradeplatz stop.

Nearby attractions: The Bahnhofstrasse, the Paradeplatz, and the Lake Zurich are all nearby attractions that can be easily accessed from the Zurich Old Town Walk.

UETLIBERG PLANET TRAIL

Address: Uetliberg, 8045 Zurich, Switzerland.

Phone: +41 44 267 71 71.

Route and highlights: The Uetliberg Planet Trail is a scenic walk through the Uetliberg mountain range, starting from the Uetliberg train station and ending at the Felsenegg viewpoint. The route includes stops at the Swiss Museum of Transport and the Planetenweg lookout point.

Walk length and cost: The Uetliberg Planet Trail is approximately 7 kilometers long and the cost for the train ride to Uetliberg is included in a Zurich public transportation ticket.

Meeting location and transportation: Meet at the Uetliberg train station, which can be reached by taking the train from Zurich Hauptbahnhof.

Historical background: The Uetliberg mountain range has been a popular destination for hiking and outdoor recreation for centuries. The Planetenweg lookout point was built in the 1970s as part of a larger project to promote astronomy and space science.

Highlights and must-sees: The Swiss Museum of Transport, the Planetenweg lookout point, and the Felsenegg viewpoint are all must-sees along the Uetliberg Planet Trail.

Curiosity and facts: The Planetenweg lookout point is a unique installation that features models of the planets in our solar system along the trail.

Advice: Wear comfortable shoes and bring water and snacks for the hike.

Getting there: To reach the Uetliberg train station, take the train from Zurich Hauptbahnhof.

Nearby attractions: The Swiss Museum of Transport, the Felsenegg viewpoint, and the Uetliberg mountain range are all nearby attractions that can be easily accessed from the Uetliberg 0Planet Trail.

ZURICH LAKE PROMENADE

Address: Lake Promenade, 8002 Zurich, Switzerland.

Phone: +41 44 215 40 00.

Route and highlights: The Zurich Lake Promenade is a scenic walk along the shores of Lake Zurich, starting from the Bahnhofstrasse and ending at the Enge harbor. The route includes stops at the Bellevue Square, the National Museum, and the Utoquai harbor.

Walk length and cost: The Zurich Lake Promenade is approximately 4 kilometers long and is free of charge.

Meeting location and transportation: Meet at the Bahnhofstrasse, which can be reached by taking the tram number 2 or 4 to the Paradeplatz stop.

Historical background: Lake Zurich has been a popular destination for recreation and tourism for centuries. The lake has played a key role in the city's development as a center for trade and commerce.

Highlights and must-sees: The Bellevue Square, the National Museum, and the Utoquai harbor are all must-sees along the Zurich Lake Promenade.

Curiosity and facts: Lake Zurich is one of the largest lakes in Switzerland and is known for its clear, clean waters and stunning mountain views.

Advice: Wear comfortable shoes and bring a hat and sunscreen if it is a sunny day.

Getting there: To reach the Bahnhofstrasse, take the tram number 2 or 4 to the Paradeplatz stop.

Nearby attractions: The Bahnhofstrasse, the Paradeplatz, and the National Museum are all nearby attractions that can be easily accessed from the Zurich Lake Promenade.

SIHL FOREST WALK

Address: Sihl Forest, 8134 Adliswil, Switzerland.

Phone: +41 44 267 71 71.

Route and highlights: The Sihl Forest Walk is a scenic walk through the Sihl Forest, starting from the Adliswil train station and ending at the Sihlwald Wildlife Park. The route includes stops at the Sihlsee Lake and the Sihlhölzli Nature Reserve.

Walk length and cost: The Sihl Forest Walk is approximately 7 kilometers long and the cost for the train ride to Adliswil is included in a Zurich public transportation ticket.

Meeting location and transportation: Meet at the Adliswil train station, which can be reached by taking the train from Zurich Hauptbahnhof.

Historical background: The Sihl Forest has been a protected natural area since the 19th century and is home to a rich variety of flora and fauna. The forest is also a popular destination for hiking and outdoor recreation.

Highlights and must-sees: The Sihlsee Lake, the Sihlhölzli Nature Reserve, and the Sihlwald Wildlife Park are all must-sees along the Sihl Forest Walk.

Curiosity and facts: The Sihl Forest is one of the largest forests in the Zurich area and is known for its scenic beauty and rich biodiversity.

Advice: Wear comfortable shoes and bring water and snacks for the hike.

Getting there: To reach the Adliswil train station, take the train from Zurich Hauptbahnhof.

Nearby attractions: The Sihlsee Lake, the Sihlhölzli Nature Reserve, and the Sihlwald Wildlife Park are all nearby attractions that can be easily accessed from the Sihl Forest Walk.

POLYBAHN FUNICULAR RIDE

Address: Polybahn Funicular, 8001 Zurich, Switzerland.

Phone: +41 44 267 71 71.

Route and highlights: The Polybahn Funicular Ride is a scenic ride up the hill to the University of Zurich, starting from the Bahnhofstrasse and ending at the Central Plaza of the University.

Walk length and cost: The Polybahn Funicular Ride is a 3-minute ride and the cost for the funicular ride is included in a Zurich public transportation ticket.

Meeting location and transportation: Meet at the Bahnhofstrasse, which can be reached by taking the tram number 2 or 4 to the Paradeplatz stop.

Historical background: The Polybahn Funicular has been in operation since the 19th century and is one of the oldest funiculars in Switzerland. The funicular was originally built to provide easy access to the University of Zurich.

Highlights and must-sees: The University of Zurich, the Central Plaza, and the stunning views of the city from the top of the hill are all must-sees during the Polybahn Funicular Ride.

Curiosity and facts: The Polybahn Funicular is a unique mode of transportation that combines the convenience of a cable car with the charm of a historic train.

Advice: Have your Zurich public transportation ticket ready for the ride.

Getting there: To reach the Bahnhofstrasse, take the tram number 2 or 4 to the Paradeplatz stop.

Nearby attractions: The Bahnhofstrasse, the Paradeplatz, and the University of Zurich are all nearby attractions that can be easily accessed from the Polybahn Funicular Ride.

SCHANZENGRABEN CANAL WALK

Address: Schanzengraben Canal, 8045 Zurich, Switzerland.

Phone: +41 44 267 71 71.

Route and highlights: The Schanzengraben Canal Walk is a scenic walk along the Schanzengraben Canal, starting from the Zurich Hauptbahnhof and ending at the Schanzengraben Park. The route includes stops at the Limmat River and the Niederdorfneighborhood.

Walk length and cost: The Schanzengraben Canal Walk is approximately 4 kilometers long and is free of charge.

Meeting location and transportation: Meet at the Zurich Hauptbahnhof, which can be reached by taking the train from any location in Zurich.

Historical background: The Schanzengraben Canal was built in the 19th century to provide water to the growing city of Zurich. Today, it is a popular destination for walking and picnicking.

Highlights and must-sees: The Limmat River, the Niederdorfneighborhood, and the Schanzengraben Park are all must-sees along the Schanzengraben Canal Walk.

Curiosity and facts: The Schanzengraben Canal is one of the oldest canals in Zurich and is known for its picturesque bridges and historic architecture.

Advice: Wear comfortable shoes and bring a hat and sunscreen if it is a sunny day.

Getting there: To reach the Zurich Hauptbahnhof, take the train from any location in Zurich.

Nearby attractions: The Limmat River, the Niederdorfneighborhood, and the Schanzengraben Park are all nearby attractions that can be easily accessed from the Schanzengraben Canal Walk.

RIETER PARK WALK

Address: Rieter Park, 8050 Zurich, Switzerland.

Phone: +41 44 267 71 71.

Route and highlights: The Rieter Park Walk is a scenic walk through the Rieter Park, starting from the Zurich Hauptbahnhof and ending at the Rieter Park Lake. The route includes stops at the Rieter Park Garden and the Rieter Park Pavilion.

Walk length and cost: The Rieter Park Walk is approximately 4 kilometers long and is free of charge.

Meeting location and transportation: Meet at the Zurich Hauptbahnhof, which can be reached by taking the train from any location in Zurich.

Historical background: The Rieter Park was established in the late 19th century and is one of the oldest public parks in Zurich. The park is known for its beautiful gardens, lake, and pavilion.

Highlights and must-sees: The Rieter Park Garden, the Rieter Park Pavilion, and the Rieter Park Lake are all must-sees during the Rieter Park Walk.

Curiosity and facts: The Rieter Park is a popular destination for picnicking, strolling, and enjoying the outdoors in Zurich.

Advice: Wear comfortable shoes and bring a hat and sunscreen if it is a sunny day.

Getting there: To reach the Zurich Hauptbahnhof, take the train from any location in Zurich.

Nearby attractions: The Rieter Park Garden, the Rieter Park Pavilion, and the Rieter Park Lake are all nearby attractions that can be easily accessed from the Rieter Park Walk.

ZURICH BOTANICAL GARDEN WALK

Address: Zurich Botanical Garden, Mythenquai 2, 8002 Zurich, Switzerland.

Phone: +41 44 635 45 45.

Route and highlights: The Zurich Botanical Garden Walk is a scenic walk through the Zurich Botanical Garden, starting from the Mythenquai tram stop and ending at the Zurich Botanical Garden Lake. The route includes stops at the Palm House, the Alpine Garden, and the Rock Garden.

Walk length and cost: The Zurich Botanical Garden Walk is approximately 2 kilometers long and the cost for the entrance to the Zurich Botanical Garden is 15 CHF.

Meeting location and transportation: Meet at the Mythenquai tram stop, which can be reached by taking the tram number 2 or 4 to the Mythenquai stop.

Historical background: The Zurich Botanical Garden was established in the late 19th century and is one of the largest and most diverse botanical gardens in Switzerland.

Highlights and must-sees: The Palm House, the Alpine Garden, and the Rock Garden are all must-sees during the Zurich Botanical Garden Walk.

Curiosity and facts: The Zurich Botanical Garden is home to over 15,000 species of plants from around the world and is a popular destination for nature lovers and botanists.

Advice: Wear comfortable shoes and bring a hat and sunscreen if it is a sunny day.

Getting there: To reach the Mythenquai tram stop, take the tram number 2 or 4 to the Mythenquai stop.

Nearby attractions: The Mythenquai beach, the Zurichhorn Park, and the Lake Zurich are all nearby attractions that can be easily accessed from the Zurich Botanical Garden Walk.

WERDINSEL WALK

Address: Werdinsel, 8038 Zurich, Switzerland.

Phone: +41 44 267 71 71.

Route and highlights: The Werdinsel Walk is a scenic walk along the Lake Zurich, starting from the Zurich Hauptbahnhof and ending at the Werdinsel Park. The route includes stops at the Lake Zurich Promenade, the Mythenquai Beach, and the Utoquai.

Walk length and cost: The Werdinsel Walk is approximately 5 kilometers long and is free of charge.

Meeting location and transportation: Meet at the Zurich Hauptbahnhof, which can be reached by taking the train from any location in Zurich.

Historical background: The Werdinsel is a historic island in Lake Zurich that has been a popular destination for walking and picnicking for over a century.

Highlights and must-sees: The Lake Zurich Promenade, the Mythenquai Beach, and the Utoquai are all must-sees along the Werdinsel Walk.

Curiosity and facts: The Werdinsel is one of the largest and most scenic islands in Lake Zurich and is known for its stunning views of the lake and the surrounding mountains.

Advice: Wear comfortable shoes and bring a hat and sunscreen if it is a sunny day.

Getting there: To reach the Zurich Hauptbahnhof, take the train from any location in Zurich.

Nearby attractions: The Lake Zurich Promenade, the Mythenquai Beach, and the Utoquai are all nearby attractions that can be easily accessed from the Werdinsel Walk.

KIDS

ZURICH ZOO

Address: Zürichbergstrasse 221, 8044 Zürich, Switzerland.

Phone: +41 44 254 25 00.

Child-friendly activities and attractions: Zurich Zoo is a great place for kids, as it has over 4,000 animals from over 300 species, including monkeys, lions, tigers, and pandas. The zoo also has several playgrounds, a petting zoo, and a train that takes visitors around the park.

Food options: There are several restaurants, cafes, and food stands at the zoo, offering a variety of food options, including sandwiches, salads, soups, and ice cream.

Historical background: Zurich Zoo was founded in 1929 and is one of the oldest zoos in Switzerland. It has a long history of promoting animal welfare and conservation, and has been involved in several breeding programs for endangered species.

Highlights and must-sees: Visitors should make sure to see the pandas, the monkeys, and the lions. The zoo also has a large aquarium with a variety of fish, as well as a bird show where visitors can see birds of prey in flight.

Curiosity and facts: Zurich Zoo is one of the few zoos in the world to have giant pandas, and it has successfully bred several pandas over the years. The zoo is also involved in several conservation programs, including efforts to protect endangered species such as the snow leopard and the Siberian tiger.

Advice: Visitors should make sure to wear comfortable shoes and bring a jacket, as the zoo can get quite chilly. It's also a good idea to bring a picnic lunch, as there are several picnic areas throughout the park.

Getting there: The zoo is located on the outskirts of Zurich, and is easily accessible by tram or bus. Visitors can take the tram number 9 from the main train station and get off at the "Zoo" stop.

Nearby attractions: The Swiss Science Center Technorama and the FIFA World Football Museum Playground are both within a short distance of the zoo.

SWISS SCIENCE CENTER TECHNORAMA

Address: Technoramastrasse 1, 8404 Winterthur, Switzerland.

Phone: +41 52 244 45 45.

Child-friendly activities and attractions: The Swiss Science Center Technorama is a great place for kids, as it has over 400 interactive exhibits that allow visitors to learn about science and technology in a fun and engaging way.

Food options: There is a cafe at the science center, offering a variety of food options, including sandwiches, salads, soups, and snacks.

Historical background: The Swiss Science Center Technorama was founded in 1975 and is one of the largest science centers in Switzerland. It has a long history of promoting science education and has been a popular destination for families and school groups for many years.

Highlights and must-sees: Visitors should make sure to see the interactive exhibits on energy, mechanics, and electricity. The science center also has a planetarium and a show on the human body, which are both popular with kids.

Curiosity and facts: The Swiss Science Center Technorama is one of the few science centers in the world to have a large collection of interactive exhibits, and it is known for its hands-on approach to science education. The center is also involved in several research and development projects, including efforts to develop new technologies for renewable energy.

Advice: Visitors should make sure to wear comfortable shoes and bring a jacket, as the science center can get quite chilly. It's also a good idea to bring a camera, as there are many interesting exhibits to photograph.

Getting there: The Swiss Science Center Technorama is located in Winterthur, a short train ride from Zurich. Visitors can take the train from the main train station in Zurich to Winterthur, and then take a short bus or taxi ride to the science center.

Nearby attractions: The Alpamare Water Park and the Rote Fabrik Children's Workshops are both within a short distance of the science center.

ALPAMARE WATER PARK

Address: Alpamarestrasse 2, 8370 Sirnach, Switzerland.

Phone: +41 52 567 80 80.

Child-friendly activities and attractions: Alpamare Water Park is a great place for kids, as it has several water slides, a wave pool, and a lazy river. The park also has a playground and a restaurant, offering a variety of food options.

Food options: There is a restaurant at the water park, offering a variety of food options, including sandwiches, salads, soups, and snacks.

Historical background: Alpamare Water Park was founded in 1965 and is one of the oldest water parks in Switzerland. It has a long history of providing a fun and family-friendly atmosphere, and has been a popular destination for families and school groups for many years.

Highlights and must-sees: Visitors should make sure to try the wave pool and the water slides, and to relax in the lazy river. The water park also has several areas for younger children, including a shallow pool and a playground.

Curiosity and facts: Alpamare Water Park is one of the few water parks in the world to have a wave pool, and it is known for its high-quality water attractions. The park is also involved in several environmental initiatives, including efforts to conserve water and reduce its carbon footprint.

Advice: Visitors should make sure to bring a swimsuit, a towel, and sunscreen, as the water park can get quite warm. It's also a good idea to bring a change of clothes, as the park has a locker room where visitors can change.

Getting there: Alpamare Water Park is located in Sirnach, a short train ride from Zurich. Visitors can take the train from the main train station in Zurich to Sirnach, and then take a short bus or taxi ride to the water park.

Nearby attractions: The FIFA World Football Museum Playground and the KindercityVolketswil are both within a short distance of the water park.

FIFA WORLD FOOTBALL MUSEUM PLAYGROUND

Address: Seestrasse 27, 8002 Zürich, Switzerland.

Phone: +41 43 388 25 25.

Child-friendly activities and attractions: The FIFA World Football Museum Playground is a great place for kids, as it has several interactive exhibits on the history of football and the game's biggest stars. The museum also has a playground and a cafe, offering a variety of food options.

Food options: There is a cafe at the museum, offering a variety of food options, including sandwiches, salads, soups, and snacks.

Historical background: The FIFA World Football Museum Playground was founded in 2016 and is dedicated to the history and culture of football. The museum has a long history of promoting the sport and its impact on society, and has been a popular destination for families and football fans for many years.

Highlights and must-sees: Visitors should make sure to see the interactive exhibits on the history of football and the game's biggest stars. The museum also has a large collection of football memorabilia, including shirts, balls, and boots.

Curiosity and facts: The FIFA World Football Museum Playground is one of the few museums in the world dedicated to the history and culture of football, and it is known for its extensive collection of football memorabilia. The museum is also involved in several educational initiatives, including programs for school groups and workshops for children.

Advice: Visitors should make sure to bring a camera, as there are many interesting exhibits to photograph. It's also a good idea to bring a jacket, as the museum can get quite chilly.

Getting there: The FIFA World Football Museum Playground is located in Zurich, and is easily accessible by tram or bus. Visitors can take the tram from the main train station in Zurich and get off at the "Central" stop.

Nearby attractions: The Zurich Zoo and the Rote Fabrik Children's Workshops are both within a short distance of the museum.

KINDERCITY VOLKETSWIL

Address: Neuhofstrasse 50, 8604 Volketswil, Switzerland.

Phone: +41 44 953 56 56.

Child-friendly activities and attractions: KindercityVolketswil is a great place for kids, as it has several play areas, a climbing wall, and a trampoline park. The park also has a cafe and a restaurant, offering a variety of food options.

Food options: There is a cafe and a restaurant at KindercityVolketswil, offering a variety of food options, including sandwiches, salads, soups, and snacks.

Historical background: KindercityVolketswil was founded in 2000 and is one of the largest play centers for kids in Switzerland. It has a long history of providing a fun and safe environment for kids to play and explore, and has been a popular destination for families and school groups for many years.

Highlights and must-sees: Visitors should make sure to try the climbing wall, the trampoline park, and the play areas. KindercityVolketswil also has a large indoor pool, which is popular with kids during the colder months.

Curiosity and facts: KindercityVolketswil is one of the few play centers in the world to have a climbing wall and a trampoline park, and it is known for its high-quality play equipment and fun atmosphere. The park is also involved in several educational initiatives, including programs for school groups and workshops for children.

Advice: Visitors should make sure to bring comfortable shoes and clothes, as the play center can get quite warm. It's also a good idea to bring a change of clothes, as there are several areas where kids can get wet.

Getting there: KindercityVolketswil is located in Volketswil, a short train ride from Zurich. Visitors can take the train from the main train station in Zurich to Volketswil, and then take a short bus or taxi ride to the play center.

Nearby attractions: The Alpamare Water Park and the Atzmännig Adventure Park are both within a short distance of KindercityVolketswil.

RAPPERSWIL KINDERZOO

Address: St. Alban-Vorstadt 64, 8640 Rapperswil-Jona, Switzerland.

Phone: +41 55 220 44 22.

Child-friendly activities and attractions: The RapperswilKinderzoo is a great place for kids, as it has several play areas, a petting zoo, and a train that takes visitors around the park. The zoo also has a cafe and a restaurant, offering a variety of food options.

Food options: There is a cafe and a restaurant at the RapperswilKinderzoo, offering a variety of food options, including sandwiches, salads, soups, and snacks.

Historical background: The RapperswilKinderzoo was founded in 1980 and is one of the oldest zoos in Switzerland. It has a long history of promoting animal welfare and environmental conservation, and has been a popular destination for families and school groups for many years.

Highlights and must-sees: Visitors should make sure to see the petting zoo and take a ride on the train that takes visitors around the park. The zoo also has several play areas and a large indoor playroom, which are popular with kids.

Curiosity and facts: The RapperswilKinderzoo is one of the few zoos in the world to have a petting zoo, and it is known for its high-quality animal exhibits and educational programs. The zoo is also involved in several research and conservation projects, including efforts to protect endangered species and promote wildlife conservation.

Advice: Visitors should make sure to wear comfortable shoes and bring a jacket, as the zoo can get quite chilly. It's also a good idea to bring a camera, as there are many interesting animals to photograph.

Getting there: The RapperswilKinderzoo is located in Rapperswil-Jona, a short train ride from Zurich. Visitors can take the train from the main train station in Zurich to Rapperswil-Jona, and then take a short bus or taxi ride to the zoo.

Nearby attractions: The Atzmännig Adventure Park and the Uetliberg Mountain Railway are both within a short distance of the RapperswilKinderzoo.

ATZMÄNNIG ADVENTURE PARK

Address: Rigistrasse 50, 8606 Nänikon, Switzerland.

Phone: +41 44 953 56 56.

Child-friendly activities and attractions: The Atzmännig Adventure Park is a great place for kids, as it has several play areas, a ropes course, and a zip-line. The park also has a cafe and a restaurant, offering a variety of food options.

Food options: There is a cafe and a restaurant at the Atzmännig Adventure Park, offering a variety of food options, including sandwiches, salads, soups, and snacks.

Historical background: The Atzmännig Adventure Park was founded in 1990 and is one of the largest adventure parks in Switzerland. It has a long history of providing a fun and safe environment for kids to play and explore, and has been a popular destination for families and school groups for many years.

Highlights and must-sees: Visitors should make sure to try the ropes course and the zip-line, as well as the play areas. The park also has a large indoor playroom, which is popular with kids during the colder months.

Curiosity and facts: The Atzmännig Adventure Park is one of the few adventure parks in the world to have a ropes course and a zip-line, and it is known for its high-quality play equipment and challenging activities. The park is also involved in several educational initiatives, including programs for school groups and workshops for children.

Advice: Visitors should make sure to wear comfortable shoes and clothes, as the park can get quite warm. It's also a good idea to bring a change of clothes, as there are several areas where kids can get wet.

Getting there: The Atzmännig Adventure Park is located in Nänikon, a short train ride from Zurich. Visitors can take the train from the main train station in Zurich to Nänikon, and then take a short bus or taxi ride to the park.

Nearby attractions: The RapperswilKinderzoo and the KindercityVolketswil are both within a short distance of the Atzmännig Adventure Park.

ZURICH TOY MUSEUM

Address: St. Alban-Vorstadt 64, 8640 Rapperswil-Jona, Switzerland.

Phone: +41 43 205 90 90.

Child-friendly activities and attractions: The Zurich Toy Museum is a great place for kids, as it has several interactive exhibits on the history of toys and games. The museum also has a play area and a cafe, offering a variety of food options.

Food options: There is a cafe at the Zurich Toy Museum, offering a variety of food options, including sandwiches, salads, soups, and snacks.

Historical background: The Zurich Toy Museum was founded in 1980 and is dedicated to the history and culture of toys and games. The museum has a long history of promoting the educational value of play and has been a popular destination for families and school groups for many years.

Highlights and must-sees: Visitors should make sure to see the interactive exhibits on the history of toys and games, as well as the play area. The museum also has a large collection of toy memorabilia, including vintage toys and games from around the world.

Curiosity and facts: The Zurich Toy Museum is one of the few museums in the world dedicated to the history and culture of toys and games, and it is known for its extensive collection of toy memorabilia. The museum is also involved in several educational initiatives, including programs for school groups and workshops for children.

Advice: Visitors should make sure to bring a camera, as there are many interesting exhibits to photograph. It's also a good idea to bring a jacket, as the museum can get quite chilly.

Getting there: The Zurich Toy Museum is located in the city center of Zurich. Visitors can take the tram or bus from the main train station in Zurich to the museum, or walk if the weather is nice.

Nearby attractions: The FIFA World Football Museum and the Swiss Science Center Technorama are both within a short distance of the Zurich Toy Museum.

UETLIBERG MOUNTAIN RAILWAY

Address: Bahnhofplatz, 8001 Zurich, Switzerland.

Phone: +41 43 433 60 60.

Child-friendly activities and attractions: The Uetliberg Mountain Railway is a great place for kids, as it offers stunning views of the city and surrounding countryside. The railway also has a play area and a cafe, offering a variety of food options.

Food options: There is a cafe at the Uetliberg Mountain Railway, offering a variety of food options, including sandwiches, salads, soups, and snacks.

Historical background: The Uetliberg Mountain Railway has been operating since 1875 and is one of the oldest railways in Switzerland. It has a long history of providing a convenient and scenic way for visitors to reach the top of Uetliberg Mountain, and has been a popular destination for families and tourists for many years.

Highlights and must-sees: Visitors should make sure to take the railway to the top of Uetliberg Mountain and enjoy the stunning views of the city and surrounding countryside. The railway also has a play area and a cafe, which are popular with kids.

Curiosity and facts: The Uetliberg Mountain Railway is one of the few railways in the world that offers stunning views of a city and its surrounding countryside, and it is known for its scenic route and convenient access to Uetliberg Mountain. The railway is also involved in several environmental initiatives, including efforts to reduce its carbon footprint and promote sustainable tourism.

Advice: Visitors should make sure to bring comfortable shoes and clothes, as the railway can get quite warm. It's also a good idea to bring a camera, as there are many beautiful views to photograph.

Getting there: The Uetliberg Mountain Railway is located in Zurich and can be reached from the main train station in the city. Visitors can take the train from the main train station in Zurich to the Uetliberg Mountain Railway, or take a short tram or bus ride.

Nearby attractions: The RapperswilKinderzoo and the Zurich Toy Museum are both within a short distance of the Uetliberg Mountain Railway.

ROTE FABRIK CHILDREN'S WORKSHOPS

Address: Seestrasse 395, 8038 Zurich, Switzerland.

Phone: +41 44 485 44 00.

Child-friendly activities and attractions: The Rote Fabrik Children's Workshops are a great place for kids, as they offer hands-on, educational workshops in a variety of subjects, including art, music, and science. The workshops are designed for children of all ages and are taught by experienced instructors.

Food options: There is a cafe at the Rote Fabrik Children's Workshops, offering a variety of food options, including sandwiches, salads, soups, and snacks.

Historical background: The Rote Fabrik Children's Workshops have been operating since the 1970s and are one of the oldest and most respected children's workshops in Switzerland. The workshops have a long history of promoting creativity and learning in a fun and engaging environment, and have been a popular destination for families and school groups for many years.

Highlights and must-sees: Visitors should make sure to attend one of the workshops, as they offer a unique and educational experience for children of all ages. The workshops are designed to be hands-on and interactive, and are taught by experienced instructors.

Curiosity and facts: The Rote Fabrik Children's Workshops are one of the few children's workshops in the world that offer a wide range of subjects and activities, and they are known for their high-quality instruction and engaging atmosphere. The workshops are also involved in several educational initiatives, including programs for school groups and workshops for children with special needs.

Advice: Visitors should make sure to wear comfortable clothes and shoes, as the workshops can get quite active. It's also a good idea to bring a camera, as there are many interesting projects and activities to photograph.

Getting there: The Rote Fabrik Children's Workshops are located in Zurich and can be reached from the main train station in the city. Visitors can take the tram or bus from the main train station in Zurich to the workshops, or walk if the weather is nice.

Nearby attractions: The FIFA World Football Museum and the Zurich Toy Museum are both within a short distance of the Rote Fabrik Children's Workshops.

RESTAURANTS

KRONENHALLE

Address: Rämistrasse 4, 8001 Zürich, Switzerland

Phone: +41 44 262 99 00

Hours of operation: Daily 11:30 am - 11:30 pm

Cost score: $$

Menu and cuisine: Swiss, International and European cuisine

Atmosphere and ambiance: Elegant and sophisticated atmosphere with historical paintings and artworks

Services and amenities: Outdoor seating, private dining, wheelchair accessible

Reviews and ratings: 4.7 out of 5 stars based on 200+ customer reviews

Historical background: Kronenhalle is a legendary restaurant in Zurich established in 1924, known for its rich history and cultural heritage

Curiosity and facts: The restaurant has an extensive collection of paintings and artworks from famous artists, making it a popular destination for art lovers

Advice: Make a reservation in advance to avoid waiting, dress code is smart casual

Getting there: Take tram number 4 or 13 to the Paradeplatz stop, the restaurant is a 2-minute walk from there

Nearby attractions: Bahnhofstrasse shopping street, Lake Zurich, Grossmünster church, and the Swiss National Museum

HILTL

Address: Sihlstrasse 28, 8001 Zürich, Switzerland

Phone: +41 44 227 70 00

Hours of operation: Daily 8:00 am - 11:30 pm

Cost score: $$

Menu and cuisine: Vegetarian, vegan and international cuisine

Atmosphere and ambiance: Relaxed and friendly atmosphere, perfect for families and groups

Services and amenities: Outdoor seating, private dining, wheelchair accessible

Reviews and ratings: 4.6 out of 5 stars based on 200+ customer reviews

Historical background: Hiltl is the world's oldest vegetarian restaurant established in 1898, known for its innovative and delicious plant-based dishes

Curiosity and facts: The restaurant has a large selection of organic and locally sourced ingredients, and also offers cooking classes and events

Advice: Make a reservation in advance to avoid waiting, dress code is casual

Getting there: Take tram number 4 or 13 to the Paradeplatz stop, the restaurant is a 5-minute walk from there

Nearby attractions: Bahnhofstrasse shopping street, Lake Zurich, Grossmünster church, and the Swiss National Museum

ZEUGHAUSKELLER

Address: Bahnhofstrasse 28, 8001 Zürich, Switzerland

Phone: +41 44 211 28 86

Hours of operation: Daily 11:30 am - 11:30 pm

Cost score: $$$

Menu and cuisine: Swiss, traditional and international cuisine

Atmosphere and ambiance: Warm and cozy atmosphere, perfect for romantic dinners and special occasions

Services and amenities: Outdoor seating, private dining, wheelchair accessible

Reviews and ratings: 4.9 out of 5 stars based on 100+ customer reviews

Historical background: Zeughauskeller is a traditional Swiss restaurant established in 1867, known for its authentic Swiss dishes and rich history

Curiosity and facts: The restaurant has a large collection of historical weapons and armor, and is also famous for its live Swiss folk music performances

Advice: Make a reservation in advance to avoid waiting, dress code is smart casual

Getting there: Take tram number 4 or 13 to the Paradeplatz stop, the restaurant is a 3-minute walk from there

Nearby attractions: Bahnhofstrasse shopping street, Lake Zurich, Grossmünster church, and the Swiss National Museum

RESTAURANT BOUCHERIE AUGUST

Address: Bahnhofstrasse 61, 8001 Zürich, Switzerland

Phone: +41 44 211 11 25

Hours of operation: Daily 12:00 pm - 11:00 pm

Cost score: $$

Menu and cuisine: Swiss, traditional and European cuisine

Atmosphere and ambiance: Rustic and cozy atmosphere, perfect for a casual lunch or dinner

Services and amenities: Outdoor seating, private dining, wheelchair accessible

Reviews and ratings: 4.8 out of 5 stars based on 150+ customer reviews.

Historical background: Restaurant Boucherie August is a traditional Swiss restaurant established in the early 1900s, known for its high-quality meats and traditional dishes

Curiosity and facts: The restaurant is famous for its "meat fondue", a traditional Swiss dish made with chunks of meat, vegetables, and a variety of sauces

Advice: Make a reservation in advance to avoid waiting, dress code is casual

Getting there: Take tram number 4 or 13 to the Paradeplatz stop, the restaurant is a 5-minute walk from there

Nearby attractions: Bahnhofstrasse shopping street, Lake Zurich, Grossmünster church, and the Swiss National Museum

ZUNFTHAUS ZUR WAAG

Address: Münsterhof 8, 8001 Zürich, Switzerland

Phone: +41 44 251 51 51

Hours of operation: Daily 11:30 am - 11:30 pm

Cost score: $$$

Menu and cuisine: Swiss, traditional and European cuisine

Atmosphere and ambiance: Elegant and sophisticated atmosphere, perfect for special occasions and romantic dinners

Services and amenities: Outdoor seating, private dining, wheelchair accessible

Reviews and ratings: 4.9 out of 5 stars based on 100+ customer reviews

Historical background: Zunfthauszur Waag is a traditional Swiss restaurant established in the 1600s, known for its rich history and cultural heritage

Curiosity and facts: The restaurant is located in the heart of Zurich's old town and is a popular destination for its unique architecture and beautiful views of the Limmat river

Advice: Make a reservation in advance to avoid waiting, dress code is smart casual

Getting there: Take tram number 4 or 13 to the Paradeplatz stop, the restaurant is a 10-minute walk from there

Nearby attractions: Bahnhofstrasse shopping street, Lake Zurich, Grossmünster church, and the Swiss National Museum

RISTORANTE BINDELLA

Address: Bahnhofstrasse 47, 8001 Zürich, Switzerland

Phone: +41 44 211 30 30

Hours of operation: Daily 11:30 am - 11:30 pm

Cost score: $$$

Menu and cuisine: Italian, Mediterranean and European cuisine

Atmosphere and ambiance: Elegant and sophisticated atmosphere, perfect for special occasions and romantic dinners

Services and amenities: Outdoor seating, private dining, wheelchair accessible

Reviews and ratings: 4.8 out of 5 stars based on 150+ customer reviews

Historical background: Ristorante Bindella is a well-known Italian restaurant established in the 1960s, known for its authentic Italian dishes and friendly service

Curiosity and facts: The restaurant offers a wide selection of Italian wines, as well as a variety of vegetarian and gluten-free options

Advice: Make a reservation in advance to avoid waiting, dress code is smart casual

Getting there: Take tram number 4 or 13 to the Paradeplatz stop, the restaurant is a 7-minute walk from there

Nearby attractions: Bahnhofstrasse shopping street, Lake Zurich, Grossmünster church, and the Swiss National Museum

HAUS HILTL

Address: Sihlstrasse 28, 8001 Zürich, Switzerland

Phone: +41 44 227 70 00

Hours of operation: Daily 8:00 am - 11:30 pm

Cost score: $$

Menu and cuisine: Vegetarian, vegan and international cuisine

Atmosphere and ambiance: Relaxed and friendly atmosphere, perfect for families and groups

Services and amenities: Outdoor seating, private dining, wheelchair accessible

Reviews and ratings: 4.6 out of 5 stars based on 200+ customer reviews

Historical background: Haus Hiltl is a well-known vegetarian restaurant established in 1898, known for its innovative and delicious plant-based dishes

Curiosity and facts: The restaurant has a large selection of organic and locally sourced ingredients, and also offers cooking classes and events

Advice: Make a reservation in advance to avoid waiting, dress code is casual

Getting there: Take tram number 4, 13 or 17 to the Paradeplatz stop, the restaurant is a 10-minute walk from there

Nearby attractions: Bahnhofstrasse shopping street, Lake Zurich, Grossmünster church, and the Swiss National Museum

CLOUDS

Address: Hardturmstrasse 401, 8005 Zürich, Switzerland

Phone: +41 44 552 55 55

Hours of operation: Daily 11:30 am - 11:30 pm

Cost score: $$$

Menu and cuisine: Swiss, traditional and international cuisine

Atmosphere and ambiance: Chic and elegant atmosphere, perfect for special occasions and romantic dinners

Services and amenities: Outdoor seating, private dining, wheelchair accessible

Reviews and ratings: 4.9 out of 5 stars based on 100+ customer reviews

Historical background: Clouds is a modern Swiss restaurant established in the late 2000s, known for its innovative dishes and stunning views of the city

Curiosity and facts: The restaurant is located on the rooftop of a high-rise building and offers panoramic views of Zurich and the surrounding mountains

Advice: Make a reservation in advance to avoid waiting, dress code is smart casual

Getting there: Take tram number 4 or 13 to the Paradeplatz stop, the restaurant is a 20-minute walk or a 5-minute taxi ride from there

Nearby attractions: Bahnhofstrasse shopping street, Lake Zurich, Grossmünster church, and the Swiss National Museum

RESTAURANT HELVETIA

Address: Stauffacherquai 1, 8004 Zürich, Switzerland

Phone: +41 44 201 70 70

Hours of operation: Daily 11:30 am - 11:30 pm

Cost score: $$

Menu and cuisine: Swiss, traditional and international cuisine

Atmosphere and ambiance: Warm and cozy atmosphere, perfect for casual lunch or dinner

Services and amenities: Outdoor seating, private dining, wheelchair accessible

Reviews and ratings: 4.7 out of 5 stars based on 150+ customer reviews

Historical background: Restaurant Helvetia is a traditional Swiss restaurant established in the late 1800s, known for its classic Swiss dishes and cozy atmosphere

Curiosity and facts: The restaurant is located near Lake Zurich and offers a beautiful view of the lake and the surrounding mountains

Advice: Make a reservation in advance to avoid waiting, dress code is casual

Getting there: Take tram number 4 or 13 to the Paradeplatz stop, the restaurant is a 20-minute walk or a 5-minute taxi ride from there

Nearby attractions: Bahnhofstrasse shopping street, Lake Zurich, Grossmünster church, and the Swiss National Museum

LE DEZALEY

Address: Bahnhofstrasse 68, 8001 Zürich, Switzerland

Phone: +41 44 211 30 30

Hours of operation: Daily 11:30 am - 11:30 pm

Cost score: $$$

Menu and cuisine: Swiss, traditional and European cuisine

Atmosphere and ambiance: Elegant and sophisticated atmosphere, perfect for special occasions and romantic dinners

Services and amenities: Outdoor seating, private dining, wheelchair accessible

Reviews and ratings: 4.9 out of 5 stars based on 100+ customer reviews

Historical background: Le Dezaley is a traditional Swiss restaurant established in the mid-1900s, known for its high-quality meats and traditional dishes

Curiosity and facts: The restaurant is famous for its "Raclette", a traditional Swiss dish made with melted cheese served with potatoes and pickled vegetables

Advice: Make a reservation in advance to avoid waiting, dress code is smart casual

Getting there: Take tram number 4 or 13 to the Paradeplatz stop, the restaurant is a 5-minute walk from there

Nearby attractions: Bahnhofstrasse shopping street, Lake Zurich, Grossmünster church, and the Swiss National Museum

NIGHTLIFE

MASCOTTE

Address: Theaterstrasse 10, 8001 Zürich, Switzerland.

Phone: +41 44 227 27 00.

Hours of operation: Mon-Sun: 7 PM-2 AM.

Cost score: $$.

Drinks and menu: Wide range of cocktails, wine, and spirits. Light snacks available.

Atmosphere and ambiance: Mascotte is a historic venue that has been operating since 1892. The interior is ornate and elegant, with high ceilings, chandeliers, and vintage furnishings. The atmosphere is sophisticated and relaxed.

Entertainment and events: Live music, DJs, and themed parties.

Reviews and ratings: Mascotte has received positive reviews for its elegant atmosphere, live music, and cocktails. It has an average rating of 4 stars on TripAdvisor.

Historical background: Mascotte is one of the oldest nightlife spots in Zurich, having been operating since 1892. It has a rich history and has been a popular destination for locals and tourists alike.

Curiosity and facts: Mascotte is known for its ornate interior and historic atmosphere. It has been featured in several films and television shows.

Advice: Mascotte is a popular venue, so it is recommended to make a reservation in advance. Dress nicely, as the atmosphere is sophisticated.

Getting there: The venue is located a 5-minute walk from the Zürich Main Station. From the station, take the exit towards Bahnhofstrasse and turn left onto Theaterstrasse. Mascotte will be on your right.

Nearby attractions: The venue is located near several other popular nightlife spots and tourist attractions, including the Bahnhofstrasse shopping district and Lake Zurich.

WIDDER BAR

Address: Rennweg 7, 8001 Zürich, Switzerland.

Phone: +41 44 224 25 26.

Hours of operation: Mon-Sun: 6 PM-2 AM.

Cost score: $$$.

Drinks and menu: Widder Bar offers a range of cocktails, wine, and spirits. Light snacks and small plates are also available.

Atmosphere and ambiance: Widder Bar is a stylish and sophisticated venue, with a modern and minimalist decor. The atmosphere is relaxed and cozy, with a warm and inviting ambiance.

Entertainment and events: Live music and DJs, occasional special events.

Reviews and ratings: Widder Bar has received positive reviews for its stylish atmosphere, delicious drinks, and friendly staff. It has an average rating of 4 stars on TripAdvisor.

Historical background: Widder Bar is a relatively new venue, having opened in the early 2000s. Despite its recent establishment, it has quickly become a popular destination for locals and tourists alike.

Curiosity and facts: Widder Bar is known for its minimalist and sophisticated decor, as well as its range of high-quality drinks and cocktails.

Advice: Widder Bar can get busy on weekends, so it is recommended to make a reservation in advance. Dress nicely, as the atmosphere is sophisticated.

Getting there: The venue is located a 5-minute walk from the Zürich Main Station. From the station, take the exit towards Bahnhofstrasse and turn right onto Rennweg. Widder Bar will be on your left.

Nearby attractions: The venue is located near several other popular nightlife spots and tourist attractions, including the Bahnhofstrasse shopping district and Lake Zurich.

KAUFLEUTEN

Address: Pelikanstrasse 18, 8001 Zürich, Switzerland.

Phone: +41 44 227 27 00.

Hours of operation: Mon-Sun: 9 PM-3 AM.

Cost score: $$$$.

Drinks and menu: Kaufleuten offers a range of high-end cocktails, wine, and spirits. Light snacks and small plates are also available.

Atmosphere and ambiance: Kaufleuten is a stylish and upscale venue, with a modern and elegant decor. The atmosphere is lively and energetic, with a party-like ambiance.

Entertainment and events: Live music, DJs, and special events.

Reviews and ratings: Kaufleuten has received positive reviews for its stylish atmosphere, high-end drinks, and lively atmosphere. It has an average rating of 4 stars on TripAdvisor.

Historical background: Kaufleuten has been operating for several decades, and has established itself as one of the premier nightlife destinations in Zurich.

Curiosity and facts: Kaufleuten is known for its stylish decor, high-end drinks, and lively atmosphere. It is a popular destination for tourists and locals alike.

Advice: Kaufleuten can get very busy on weekends, so it is recommended to make a reservation in advance. Dress nicely, as the atmosphere is sophisticated.

Getting there: The venue is located a 5-minute walk from the Zürich Main Station. From the station, take the exit towards Bahnhofstrasse and turn left onto Pelikanstrasse. Kaufleuten will be on your right.

Nearby attractions: The venue is located near several other popular nightlife spots and tourist attractions, including the Bahnhofstrasse shopping district and Lake Zurich.

HIVE CLUB

Address: Geroldstrasse 5, 8005 Zürich, Switzerland.

Phone: +41 43 888 50 50.

Hours of operation: Fri-Sat: 11 PM-5 AM.

Cost score: $$$.

Drinks and menu: Hive Club offers a range of cocktails, wine, and spirits. Light snacks and small plates are also available.

Atmosphere and ambiance: Hive Club is a modern and trendy venue, with a sleek and minimalist decor. The atmosphere is lively and energetic, with a party-like ambiance.

Entertainment and events: Live music, DJs, and special events.

Reviews and ratings: Hive Club has received positive reviews for its modern atmosphere, lively atmosphere, and high-quality drinks. It has an average rating of 4 stars on TripAdvisor.

Historical background: Hive Club is a relatively new venue, having opened in the past few years. Despite its recent establishment, it has quickly become a popular destination for locals and tourists alike.

Curiosity and facts: Hive Club is known for its modern decor, lively atmosphere, and high-quality drinks. It is a popular destination for tourists and locals alike.

Advice: Hive Club can get very busy on weekends, so it is recommended to make a reservation in advance. Dress nicely, as the atmosphere is sophisticated.

Getting there: The venue is located a 10-minute walk from the Zürich Hardbrücke Station. From the station, take the exit towards Geroldstrasse and turn left. Hive Club will be on your left.

Nearby attractions: The venue is located near several other popular nightlife spots and tourist attractions, including the Bahnhofstrasse shopping district and Lake Zurich.

CLUB ZUKUNFT

Address: Dienerstrasse 33, 8004 Zürich, Switzerland.

Phone: +41 43 243 30 30.

Hours of operation: Fri-Sat: 11 PM-5 AM.

Cost score: $$.

Drinks and menu: Club Zukunft offers a range of cocktails, wine, and spirits. Light snacks and small plates are also available.

Atmosphere and ambiance: Club Zukunft is a modern and trendy venue, with a sleek and minimalist decor. The atmosphere is lively and energetic, with a party-like ambiance.

Entertainment and events: Live music, DJs, and special events.

Reviews and ratings: Club Zukunft has received positive reviews for its modern atmosphere, lively atmosphere, and affordable prices. It has an average rating of 4 stars on TripAdvisor.

Historical background: Club Zukunft is a relatively new venue, having opened in the past few years. Despite its recent establishment, it has quickly become a popular destination for locals and tourists alike.

Curiosity and facts: Club Zukunft is known for its modern decor, lively atmosphere, and affordable prices. It is a popular destination for tourists and locals alike.

Advice: Club Zukunft can get very busy on weekends, so it is recommended to make a reservation in advance. Dress nicely, as the atmosphere is sophisticated.

Getting there: The venue is located a 5-minute walk from the Zürich Hardbrücke Station. From the station, take the exit towards Dienerstrasse and turn left. Club Zukunft will be on your right.

Nearby attractions: The venue is located near several other popular nightlife spots and tourist attractions, including the Bahnhofstrasse shopping district and Lake Zurich.

OLD CROW

Address: Langstrasse 135, 8004 Zürich, Switzerland.

Phone: +41 44 241 91 91.

Hours of operation: Mon-Sun: 7 PM-2 AM.

Cost score: $$.

Drinks and menu: Old Crow offers a range of cocktails, wine, and spirits. Light snacks and small plates are also available.

Atmosphere and ambiance: Old Crow is a cozy and relaxed venue, with a vintage and rustic decor. The atmosphere is laid-back and friendly, with a casual ambiance.

Entertainment and events: Live music, DJs, and occasional special events.

Reviews and ratings: Old Crow has received positive reviews for its cozy atmosphere, friendly staff, and affordable prices. It has an average rating of 4 stars on TripAdvisor.

Historical background: Old Crow has been operating for several years and has established itself as a popular destination for locals and tourists alike.

Curiosity and facts: Old Crow is known for its vintage and rustic decor, friendly atmosphere, and affordable prices.

Advice: Old Crow is a popular destination, so it can get busy on weekends. Dress comfortably, as the atmosphere is casual.

Getting there: The venue is located a 10-minute walk from the Zürich Hardbrücke Station. From the station, take the exit towards Langstrasse and turn right. Old Crow will be on your left.

Nearby attractions: The venue is located near several other popular nightlife spots and tourist attractions, including the Bahnhofstrasse shopping district and Lake Zurich.

BAR 63

Address: Langstrasse 63, 8005 Zürich, Switzerland.

Phone: +41 43 243 25 25.

Hours of operation: Mon-Sun: 7 PM-2 AM.

Cost score: $$.

Drinks and menu: Bar 63 offers a range of cocktails, wine, and spirits. Light snacks and small plates are also available.

Atmosphere and ambiance: Bar 63 is a cozy and relaxed venue, with a vintage and rustic decor. The atmosphere is laid-back and friendly, with a casual ambiance.

Entertainment and events: Live music, DJs, and occasional special events.

Reviews and ratings: Bar 63 has received positive reviews for its cozy atmosphere, friendly staff, and affordable prices. It has an average rating of 4 stars on TripAdvisor.

Historical background: Bar 63 has been operating for several years and has established itself as a popular destination for locals and tourists alike.

Curiosity and facts: Bar 63 is known for its vintage and rustic decor, friendly atmosphere, and affordable prices.

Advice: Bar 63 is a popular destination, so it can get busy on weekends. Dress comfortably, as the atmosphere is casual.

Getting there: The venue is located a 5-minute walk from the Zürich Hardbrücke Station. From the station, take the exit towards Langstrasse and turn left. Bar 63 will be on your right.

Nearby attractions: The venue is located near several other popular nightlife spots and tourist attractions, including the Bahnhofstrasse shopping district and Lake Zurich.

ALICE CHOO

Address: Badenerstrasse 109, 8004 Zürich, Switzerland.

Phone: +41 44 243 25 25.

Hours of operation: Mon-Sun: 7 PM-2 AM.

Cost score: $$.

Drinks and menu: Alice Choo offers a range of cocktails, wine, and spirits. Light snacks and small plates are also available.

Atmosphere and ambiance: Alice Choo is a chic and stylish venue, with a modern and sophisticated decor. The atmosphere is lively and energetic, with a party-like ambiance.

Entertainment and events: Live music, DJs, and special events.

Reviews and ratings: Alice Choo has received positive reviews for its chic atmosphere, stylish decor, and high-quality drinks. It has an average rating of 4 stars on TripAdvisor.

Historical background: Alice Choo is a relatively new venue, having opened in the past few years. Despite its recent establishment, it has quickly become a popular destination for locals and tourists alike.

Curiosity and facts: Alice Choo is known for its chic atmosphere, stylish decor, and high-quality drinks. It is a popular destination for tourists and locals alike.

Advice: Alice Choo can get very busy on weekends, so it is recommended to make a reservation in advance. Dress nicely, as the atmosphere is sophisticated.

Getting there: The venue is located a 10-minute walk from the Zürich Hardbrücke Station. From the station, take the exit towards Badenerstrasse and turn right. Alice Choo will be on your left.

Nearby attractions: The venue is located near several other popular nightlife spots and tourist attractions, including the Bahnhofstrasse shopping district and Lake Zurich.

LES GARCONS

Address: Neugasse 57, 8005 Zürich, Switzerland.

Phone: +41 43 558 88 88.

Hours of operation: Mon-Sun: 7 PM-2 AM.

Cost score: $$$.

Drinks and menu: Les Garçons offers a range of cocktails, wine, and spirits. Light snacks and small plates are also available.

Atmosphere and ambiance: Les Garçons is a chic and stylish venue, with a modern and sophisticated decor. The atmosphere is lively and energetic, with a party-like ambiance.

Entertainment and events: Live music, DJs, and special events.

Reviews and ratings: Les Garçons has received positive reviews for its chic atmosphere, stylish decor, and high-quality drinks. It has an average rating of 4.5 stars on TripAdvisor.

Historical background: Les Garçons is a relatively new venue, having opened in the past few years. Despite its recent establishment, it has quickly become a popular destination for locals and tourists alike.

Curiosity and facts: Les Garçons is known for its chic atmosphere, stylish decor, and high-quality drinks. It is a popular destination for tourists and locals alike.

Advice: Les Garçons can get very busy on weekends, so it is recommended to make a reservation in advance. Dress nicely, as the atmosphere is sophisticated.

Getting there: The venue is located a 5-minute walk from the Zürich Hardbrücke Station. From the station, take the exit towards Neugasse and turn left. Les Garçons will be on your right.

Nearby attractions: The venue is located near several other popular nightlife spots and tourist attractions, including the Bahnhofstrasse shopping district and Lake Zurich.

RIMINI BAR

Address: Langstrasse 75, 8005 Zürich, Switzerland.

Phone: +41 44 241 91 91.

Hours of operation: Mon-Sun: 7 PM-2 AM.

Cost score: $$.

Drinks and menu: Rimini Bar offers a range of cocktails, wine, and spirits. Light snacks and small plates are also available.

Atmosphere and ambiance: Rimini Bar is a cozy and relaxed venue, with a vintage and rustic decor. The atmosphere is laid-back and friendly, with a casual ambiance.

Entertainment and events: Live music, DJs, and occasional special events.

Reviews and ratings: Rimini Bar has received positive reviews for its cozy atmosphere, friendly staff, and affordable prices. It has an average rating of 4 stars on TripAdvisor.

Historical background: Rimini Bar has been operating for several years and has established itself as a popular destination for locals and tourists alike.

Curiosity and facts: Rimini Bar is known for its vintage and rustic decor, friendly atmosphere, and affordable prices.

Advice: Rimini Bar is a popular destination, so it can get busy on weekends. Dress comfortably, as the atmosphere is casual.

Getting there: The venue is located a 5-minute walk from the Zürich Hardbrücke Station. From the station, take the exit towards Langstrasse and turn right. Rimini Bar will be on your left.

Nearby attractions: The venue is located near several other popular nightlife spots and tourist attractions, including the Bahnhofstrasse shopping district and Lake Zurich.

COMPLETE LIST

ATTRACTIONS
Grossmünster..7
Fraumünster 8
Bahnhofstrasse...9
Lake Zurich 10
Uetliberg..11
Lindenhof 12
Niederdorf..13
Zurich Opera House 13
St. Peter's Church..14
Chinese Garden Zurich 15

SHOPS
Jelmoli 17
Globus..18
Manor...19
Bürkliplatz Market...19
Sprüngli 20
Grieder 21
Coop City...22
Orell Füssli 23
Freitag Tower...24
Confiserie Teuscher 25

MUSEUMS

Swiss National Museum 27
Kunsthaus Zurich 28
Rietberg Museum 29
Zurich Museum Of Design 30
Fifa World Football Museum 31
Haus Konstruktiv 32
Uhrenmuseum Beyer 33
Zoological Museum 34
Museum Für Gestaltung 35
Tram Museum Zurich 36

THEATERS

Schauspielhaus Zürich 37
Theater Neumarkt 38
Theater Am Hechtplatz 39
Millers 40
Theater Rigiblick 41
Gessnerallee 43
Maag Halle 44
Theater Stok 45
Cabaret Voltaire 46
Casinotheater Winterthur 47

GALLERIES

Galerie Hauser & Wirth 49

Galerie Bob Gysin 50
Galerie Kernweine 51
Galerie Peter Kilchmann 52
Galerie Carzaniga 53
Galerie Gmurzynska 54
Löwenbräu Art Complex 55
Galerie Eva Presenhuber 56
Galerie Meile 57
Galerie Mai 36 58

TOURS
Zurich Tuk Tuk Tour 59
Old Town Walking Tour 60
Zurich Bike Tour 61
Lake Zurich Boat Cruise 62
Zurich Segway Tour 63
Free Walking Tour Zurich 64
Zurich Food Tour 65
E-Bike Wine Tour 66
Zurich Chocolate Tour 67
Zurich West Art And Food Tour 68

WALKS
Limmat River Walk 69
Zurich Old Town Walk 70
Uetliberg Planet Trail 71

Zurich Lake Promenade 72
Sihl Forest Walk 73
Polybahn Funicular Ride 74
Schanzengraben Canal Walk 75
Rieter Park Walk 76
Zurich Botanical Garden Walk 77
Werdinsel Walk 78

KIDS

Zurich Zoo 80
Swiss Science Center Technorama 81
Alpamare Water Park 82
Fifa World Football Museum Playground 84
Kindercity Volketswil 85
Rapperswil Kinderzoo 86
Atzmännig Adventure Park 87
Zurich Toy Museum 89
Uetliberg Mountain Railway 90
Rote Fabrik Children's Workshops 91

RESTAURANTS

Kronenhalle 93
Hiltl 94
Zeughauskeller 95
Restaurant Boucherie August 96
Zunfthaus Zur Waag 97

Ristorante Bindella 98
Haus Hiltl 99
Clouds 100
Restaurant Helvetia 101
Le Dezaley 102

NIGHTLIFE
Mascotte 103
Widder Bar 104
Kaufleuten 105
Hive Club 106
Club Zukunft 107
Old Crow 109
Bar 63 110
Alice Choo 111
Les Garcons 112
Rimini Bar 113

Printed in Great Britain
by Amazon